Lyford P. Edwards

THE NATURAL HISTORY OF REVOLUTION

THE HERITAGE OF SOCIOLOGY

A Series Edited by Morris Janowitz

Lyford P. Edwards

THE NATURAL HISTORY
OF REVOLUTION

With a Foreword by
MORRIS JANOWITZ

THE UNIVERSITY OF CHICAGO PRESS

CHICAGO AND LONDON

ISBN: 0–226–18490–0 (clothbound);
0–226–18491–9 (paperbound)

Library of Congress Catalog Card Number: 77–127821

THE UNIVERSITY OF CHICAGO PRESS, CHICAGO 60637
The University of Chicago Press, Ltd., London

Contents

Contents

Foreword

The Natural History of Revolution by Lyford P. Edwards appeared in 1927, as part of the University of Chicago Sociological Series, in which the monographs of the "Chicago school" were published. The study was one of the first detached sociological analyses of revolution prepared in the United States. It was immediately recognized as a seminal volume and for more than a decade was widely cited because of the author's effort to present a series of related propositions about the "natural history" of revolution.

Lyford P. Edwards did not write further on revolution but devoted himself to his teaching at Saint Stephens (later Bard) College, a school remote from the centers of American academic life. As a result the book had a strange fate. It slowly lost prominence to another volume on the subject, *The Anatomy of Revolution*, published a decade later, in 1938, by Crane Brinton, the Harvard University historian. The Edwards book, however, had strongly influenced Brinton's thinking, and it was through *The Anatomy of Revolution* that Edwards's ideas about the natural history of revolution and the various stages of a revolution gained wider currency. In fact, Brinton was generous enough to describe the Edwards study in his annotated bibliography as "unpretentious, suggestive, tentative. One of the best introductions to the subject available in English." It is particularly revealing that Brinton should have added the comment, "admirably free from special pleading." As late as the mid-1930s the scholarly study of revolution was still a struggling enterprise, and Edwards stood as an intellectual pioneer.

The Natural History of Revolution was a direct product of the intellectual ferment of the Chicago school during the period before and during the First World War. Edwards, an Episcopal priest, had taken his Ph.D. in church history at the University of Chicago Divinity School at a time when there were close connections between the Department of Sociology and the Divinity School. As during the political and social unrest of the 1960s, students of religion turned to the social sciences, and particularly to sociology, in the hope of finding new sources of stimulation.

Edwards presumably listened to Robert E. Park's lectures and was impressed with his interest in collective behavior. A number of important empirical studies on collective behavior and social movements were being written under Park's stimulation; these included Ernest T. Hiller's book *The Strike.* Edwards also worked with Walter L. Dorn, of the Department of History. The practice of collaboration between historians and sociologists was already developing.

From Park's introduction to the original edition and from personal communication with Edwards, the circumstances involved in writing this book can readily be reconstructed. Park read with great interest a short paper by Edwards entitled "Mechanisms of Revolution," which appeared in the *Bulletin* of Saint Stephens College. The notion of a "comparative history" offered by Frederick J. Teggart and part of the thinking of Edwards greatly appealed to Park. Edwards has recorded Park's reaction to his article. "He thought it should be expanded to book size. I did not get very enthusiastic, but he kept after me and I finally agreed to do it. He gave me suggestions and on a weekend spent at my home in Stamford, Connecticut, he and I did a rough draft of the book. He read the proof on some of it. Without his insistence and encouragement it would never have been written."[1] This was, of course, a familiar role for Park.

The style of writing and the historical documentation in *The Natural History of Revolution* may well appear outmoded. But the implicit framework and the particular propositions focus

---

[1]   Personal communication from Lyford P. Edwards, 13 May 1969.

directly on the essential substance of contemporary research on revolution. Edwards offers a framework built on the sequential phases of a revolution which supplied the basic argument for Crane Brinton. He saw revolutionary movements as starting slowly and requiring a relatively long period of development. The initial phases of the revolution are led by moderates and after preliminary success, the radicals seize power. In turn, this second phase gives way to a new equilibrium of a more moderated outcome.

Edwards offers a variety of hypotheses about the problematic issues in this type of natural history. For example, and illustratively, the outbreak of violence implies that the underlying economic, social, and political processes of change are clearly in motion. The revolutionary situation is not the result of deprivation, which is, of course, an essential prerequisite, but the result of a crisis of legitimacy—that is, "legitimate aspirations and ideals are being repressed or perverted" (p. 30). He emphasizes the role of the "outsider" and the "stranger" in supplying symbolic leadership, and of the necessity of enlisting elements of the existing upper class if the revolution is to succeed. The intellectuals are a key in providing this transfer of allegiance.

Edwards is explicit in offering his observations about the social and economic conditions under which revolutionary activity increases, and there is a body of research literature subsequently collected to support his notions. The militant phase develops when there is a "marked increase of wealth, intelligence, and power in the repressed portion of society. . . . With this gradual increase of their wealth and knowledge comes a corresponding change in their beliefs and opinions, sentiments and feelings. Conditions of life which were previously tolerable become intolerable" (pp. 33 and 34). But Edwards presses the analysis further, anticipating the work of many political scientists and psychologists. "An essential step in the development of revolution is the gradual concentration of public dissatisfaction upon some one institution and the persons representing it" (p. 46). Edwards does not have a theory of mass psychology or of a cultural analysis of symbols, but these aspects are not overlooked.

The range of topics covered is immense even if none is

probed in depth. He deals with the role of the peasants in revolutionary situations, and with their primary interest in land reform. His analysis of the greater role of the peasants in the French versus the British revolution foreshadows the type of analysis presented by Barrington Moore in his *Social Origins of Dictatorship and Democracy* (p. 81). He deals with the symbolic aspects of riots, indicating that the management of riots is a symbolic key to the effectiveness of ruling classes and, in turn, that through rioting revolutionary groups can demonstrate the real and imputed impotence of existing leadership (p. 107). In his analysis of armed revolutionary conflict, he stresses as essential elements the fusion of radical symbols with national patriotism in a manner which is directly relevant to the understanding of contemporary wars of national liberation (p. 162).

The dynamics of violent revolutionary situations rest on the delicate position of the moderates between the conservatives and the radicals. Change is propelled by the moderates' destruction of the conservative elements, thus leaving the path open for the assumption of power by the radicals. Edwards points to the pressures of economic chaos as forcing a new postradical equilibrium. But here his analysis may be overstated, because revolutionary regimes have increasingly demonstrated their capacity to solve problems of economic development, even though the social costs may be high, or, at the least, they have demonstrated their ability to ride out instabilities for a long period of time.

Fundamentally, Edwards sees revolution as a "collective action" in which underlying social context interacts with the conscious efforts of intellectuals and dedicated agents of change. In other words the basic notion of "natural history" is designed to focus attention not only on underlying technological, economic, and political discontinuities which produce the preconditions for revolutionary change. By drawing on notions of Robert E. Park about communications and symbolism, the application of the concept of natural history to the study of revolutions is designed to explore the collective response to these discontinuities. The intellectual goal thereby is to avoid a mechanistic formulation in which the results of a revolutionary situation are predetermined. To the contrary, the outcomes of revolutions—especially violent revolutions—are problematic, and the tasks of the social investigator are to determine the intervening variables which fashion the form and content of the revolution itself and its outcome.

The book in its own way is an expression of what has come to be called macrosociology, or comparative macrosociology. Edwards samples revolutionary situations in a variety of historical and cross-national settings. The execution of the method at some points may appear arbitrary and incomplete, but the fact that he searches for situations in which revolutions failed to take place is crucial. His basic model of the stages of revolution is not the objective for him; these stages serve as a framework for understanding and exploring particular revolutions in specific historical settings. The end product of the intellectual endeavor is not a set of generalizations, but rather an explication of concrete historical processes.

Although Edwards's book has had an important impact on scholarship, the effect has been indirect and without full recognition of his efforts and those of his collaborators. Edwards deserves greater recognition. This new edition in The Heritage of Sociology series, however, has as its main purpose to point out again that the study of conflict and revolutions is a generic aspect of the history of sociological scholarship in the United States.

MORRIS JANOWITZ

February 1970

Introduction

In May, 1923, there appeared over the signature of Lyford P. Edwards, and in the *Bulletin* of St. Stephens College at Annandale-on-Hudson, a little paper of some seven pages, entitled "Mechanisms of Revolution." What distinguished this paper from most other literature on this subject was its emphasis—as its title suggests—on what may be called the "phenomenal" and "naturalistic" as contrasted with the "historical" aspects of these · catastrophic changes in social life and institutions that we call "revolutions."

This paper, in short, is an attempt to give an outline, not a history, not even—to use a term made familiar by Frederick J. Teggart—"a comparative history," but a natural history, of revolution. Revolutions, it is here assumed, are describable in general and in conceptual terms; they may even turn out to be, like earthquakes, measurably predictable. The "mechanisms" involved, of course, are social and mental.

In substance, the present volume is an expansion of this first brief sketch. Naturally the whole conception of the subject has been enlarged and modified in the process of elaboration and in the attempt to check up, by reference to concrete historical materials, notions that in the outline are described abstractly and formally.

The literature of revolution has already familiarized us with the notion that revolutions can be, and in fact have been, systematically provoked and incited. These larger and more inclusive social movements can be carried on and directed in ways and by methods which are, to be sure, different, but at any rate comparable with those employed in labor strikes. Revolution has, in fact, been conceived as a form of strike, a "general strike," so called. As strikes, local in origin, become more widely extended, involving wider areas of the organized and institutional life of the community, they assume the character of revolutions.

All this suggests that perhaps there is already in existence a revolutionary tradition and a body of more or less clearly defined and generally accepted tactics for carrying on revolutionary agitation and conducting revolutionary movements. But if there are recognized tactics for conducting revolutions, and if there is, so to speak, a revolutionary technique, this, of itself, presupposes the existence of something generic and typical in these movements —something that can be described in general terms. It presupposes, in short, the existence of materials for a scientific account of revolution, since science—natural science—in the long run is little more than a description in conceptual terms of the processes by which events take place, together with explanations which permit events to be predicted and controlled. Every attempt to control social change may be regarded as a kind of social experiment. A description and an interpretation of these experiments is precisely the business of the social sciences.

A good deal that has been written concerning revolution has emphasized the difference between social changes which are revolutionary and those which are evolutionary. In such cases discussion is centered about the value and the legitimacy of evolutionary as over against revolutionary change. With this matter of the relative desirability of one form of social change over another, neither this nor any other scientific study is immediately concerned. What a naturalistic account of revolutions seeks is such a description of the revolutionary phenomena as will tell us not what ought to happen, but what very probably will happen; not what we should do, but what we can do, in a given situation. If revolutions can be made, they can at the same time be prevented; and a study of the conditions under which ordinarily and naturally they seem to arise should throw some light on the way they have been and can be dealt with. Furthermore, the contrast between evolutionary and revolutionary changes, from the point of view of this volume at least, is fictitious and misleading. It is the very first assumption of the natural history of revolutions that these catastrophes are themselves the product of an evolutionary process. A natural history, in fact, is nothing more nor less than an account of an evolutionary process—a process by which not the individual but the type evolves. Revolution is not, it seems to me, adequately characterized as change, either progressive or catastrophic, but rather as a more specific type of what we may describe as "collective action." Like war, revolution is a movement which invariably, in its latter phases at any rate, inflames the imagination and projects itself in advance of action, in the form of an ideal. This is not true, of course, of every form of social change. Revolution, as the author somewhere suggests, is to be compared and contrasted with such other types of collective action as reform and fashion, perhaps also with migration. All these forms of change are dominated and controlled by some kind of collective representation, to use Lévy-Bruhl's expression. It is the existence of this collective representation which converts change into action.

As a matter of fact, excepting war, religion, and romantic love, nothing in ordinary human experience has so inflamed the imagination of men, encouraged so many romantic illusions, or broken so completely with the ordinary routine of existence, as has been true of revolution. Wars have been more destructive, but wars have been defensive as well as aggressive; they have been carried on to gain territory or to hold it to achieve political power or to maintain it. It is only when wars have been fought to realize some romantic ideal—freedom, for example—that they have changed profoundly and immediately the traditional aims and tendencies of our common life. It is because, and in so far as, revolutions have been dominated by collective representations, that they set themselves off as special forms of social change. They are a type, as I have already said, of collective action.

On the other hand, revolutions, as Mr. Edwards has pointed out, are invariably the effects of long and silent changes which have been felt but not fairly faced nor fully understood. It is only in the later stages, when these changes have projected themselves into the consciousness of men and proclaimed themselves in banners and slogans and utopian myths, that they have assumed the forms of a revolution, as common sense conceives it.

In their earlier stages revolutions may be compared to industrial and business crises. When industrial and business crises get into the field of politics they assume the character, sometimes, at any rate, of revolutions. Revolutions, in fact, are frequently merely the reverberation in politics of prolonged industrial and economic depressions. It is one of the conclusions of this volume, with which, I might add, I am not at present in perfect and complete agreement, that all revolutions have been and will continue to be economic in their origin. It follows that if we would control the economic and industrial processes, revolution as a social phenomenon would cease to exist.

Like industrial crises, revolutions, when they do occur, tend to describe, in their evolution, a characteristic cycle of change. Every social change that is capable of description in conceptual terms, will have, as in this case, its characteristic cycle. This is one of the presuppositions upon which this study is based. As a matter of scientific method, this description of the cycle seems to be the first step in the analysis and description of social change everywhere. It is, on the whole, all, or nearly all, that the present study has attempted to do. In fact, it is as far, or nearly as far, as any systematic study has attempted to go. At most these studies have described, or sought to describe, the revolutionary cycle. It would seem that what remains to be done is to reduce this revolutionary cycle not merely to a conceptual but to a temporal sequence, one in which the series of changes through which every revolutionary movement tends to pass are so determined and accurately described that they can be measured in temporal units. This involves a much more complete analysis of revolutionary processes than thus far has been anywhere measurably achieved. It is perhaps an impossible task, demanding a precision that is quite beyond the present limits of the social sciences. No such precision is attempted here. This volume should serve, however, as an introduction to a field in which much has been written but in which there has been very little systematic observation. If its conclusions, considering the nature of the problem, seem premature or not wholly justified by all the known facts, nevertheless it has at the very least defined for us the task which remains to be done.

ROBERT E. PARK

University of Chicago

Preface

The AUTHOR wishes to acknowledge his indebtedness to the members of his 1924 class in modern radicalism who divided among them the task of compiling a great mass of historical data some of which has been used in this book. He is more especially obliged to Mr. E. B. Woodruff for making a comparative table of the data compiled by this class. He is indebted to Dr. Bernard I. Bell, president of St. Stephen's College, for constant stimulus and encouragement.

His thanks are due to Dr. Walter L. Dorn, of the History Department of the University of Chicago, who read the manuscript and made various helpful emendations to the historical references. Thanks are also due to Dr. Louis Wirth, who compiled the Bibliography, and to Helen Gray Edwards, who prepared the copy for publication.

Above all, the writer is under manifold obligations to Professor Robert E. Park, who has given his constant help and has written the Introduction.

Some of the material contained in this book has appeared in various periodicals. Much of it has come to the author through conversations with persons too numerous to name, but to whom collectively he expresses his thanks.

L. P. EDWARDS

St. Stephen's College
Annandale, N.Y., 1927

CHAPTER I

REVOLUTION AND EVOLUTION

The most fundamental fact about human society is that
it changes. The rate of change is sometimes greater and
sometimes less, but change—at some rate—is perpetual.
Societies commonly thought of as static are so only in appearance. This appearance is deceptive, and the deception
is due to the ignorance of the observer. A very slight ac-
quaintance with the history of China, Japan, or India is
sufficient to dissipate any idea of the "Unchanging East."
There is a permanence of social order in the Orient which
Westerners mistake for petrifaction. The reading of an en-
cyclopedia article on porcelain or printing is all that is
needed to correct this mistake.

Though social change is continuous, it is seldom or never
uniform. Certain elements of culture develop or decay more
rapidly than others. There is every possible rate of accelera-
tion and retardation. Civilizations decline and die as surely
as they arise and flourish. The mechanisms which cause social change are exceedingly numerous. They have never
been studied and classified with any degree of completeness.
The great social revolutions which seem to cut across the
historical continuity of Western civilization are not unique
phenomena. They are simply a specialized type of change.
They are one form of a great number of forms of social al-
teration—one mechanism out of the many that operate to
change human society. Other mechanisms are fads, fashions,
crazes, panics, elections, revivals, crusades, insurrections,

wars, scientific discoveries, and mechanical inventions. There is no agreement among writers on the subject of revolutions on a definition.[1] The one adopted in this study as a working hypothesis is: A change brought about not necessarily by force and violence, whereby one system of legality is terminated and another originated.

The scientific study of collective behavior takes as its point of departure some theory of human motivation. The formulation which underlies this investigation is that of the four wishes of Thomas, which has gained wide acceptance. This theory asserts that human beings manifest four elemental kinds of wishes. These four classes of wishes are: (1) the wish for new experience; (2) the wish for security; (3) the wish for recognition; and (4) the wish for response.[2]

[1] For a concise discussion of current definitions of "revolution," see Dale Yoder, "Current Definitions of Revolution," *American Journal of Sociology*, XXXII (November, 1926), 433–41.

[2] "1. The desire for new experience is seen in simple form in the prowling and meddling activities of the child, and the love of adventure and travel in the boy and the man. It ranges in moral quality from the pursuit of game and the pursuit of pleasure to the pursuit of knowledge and the pursuit of ideals. It is found equally in the vagabond and in the scientific explorer. Novels, theatres, motion pictures, etc., are means of satisfying this desire vicariously, and their popularity is a sign of the elemental force of this desire.

"In its pure form the desire for new experience implies motion, change, danger, instability, social irresponsibility. The individual dominated by it shows a tendency to disregard prevailing standards and group interests. He may be a complete failure, on account of his instability; or a conspicuous success, if he converts his experiences into social values—puts them in the form of a poem, makes of them a contribution to science, etc.

"2. The desire for security is opposed to the desire for new experience. It implies avoidance of danger and death, caution, conservatism. Incorporation in an organization (family, community, state) provides the greatest security. In certain animal societies (e.g., the ants) the organization and co-operation are very rigid. Similarly among the peasants of Europe, represented by our immigrant groups, all lines of behavior are predetermined for the individual by tradition. In such a group the individual is secure so long

A stable and contented society is one in which these four elemental wishes find adequate expression through existing institutions and practices. An unstable and revolutionary society is one in which they do not. All revolution may thus be conceived of as due to the repression of one or more of these elemental wishes, and the violence of any revolution is, it is assumed, proportional to the amount of such repres-

---

as the group organization is secure, but evidently he shows little originality or creativeness.

"3. The desire for recognition expresses itself in devices for securing distinction in the eyes of the public. A list of the different modes of seeking recognition would be very long. It would include courageous behavior, showing off through ornament and dress, the pomp of kings, the display of opinions and knowledge, the possession of special attainments—in the arts, for example. It is expressed alike in arrogance and in humility, even in martyrdom. Certain modes of seeking recognition we define as 'vanity,' others as 'ambition.' The 'will to power' belongs here. Perhaps there has been no spur to human activity so keen and no motive so naïvely avowed as the desire for 'undying fame,' and it would be difficult to estimate the rôle the desire for recognition has played in the creation of social values.

"4. The desire for response is a craving, not for the recognition of the public at large, but for the more intimate appreciation of individuals. It is exemplified in mother-love (touch plays an important rôle in this connection), in romantic love, family affection, and other personal attachments. Homesickness and loneliness are expressions of it. Many of the devices for securing recognition are used also in securing response.

"Apparently these four classes comprehend all the positive wishes. Such attitudes as anger, fear, hate and prejudice are attitudes toward those objects which may frustrate a wish.

"Our hopes, fears, inspirations, joys, sorrows, are bound up with these wishes and issue from them. There is, of course, a kaleidoscopic mingling of wishes throughout life, and a single given act may contain a plurality of them. Thus when a peasant emigrates to America he may expect to have a good time and learn many things (new experiences), to make a fortune (greater security), to have a higher social standing on his return (recognition), and to induce a certain person to marry him (response)."—See W. I. Thomas, "The Person and His Wishes," in Park and Burgess, *Introduction to the Science of Sociology* (University of Chicago Press, 1924), pp. 488–90.

sion.[1] A study of the life-histories of the members of any violently revolutionary group will show numerous instances of the repression of these elemental wishes by the practices and institutions characteristic of the society in which the revolutionists live. A revolution may be regarded as one of those mutations of society which involve the destruction of those institutions of a given society which interfere with the attainment of one or more of the four elemental human wishes.

The practice of referring to biological analogies in the study of human social life has been so much abused by the early writers on sociology that anyone employing it today feels constrained to apologize for doing so. Nevertheless, if the biological analogy be employed, as it should, to denote resemblance without affinity, it has its place. It is a useful device in exposition and especially useful in clarifying our conceptions of social phenomena. With this preliminary caveat, a comparison of biological and social processes may, perhaps, be not unprofitable.

The nature of evolution is such that one dominant species of plant or animal does not evolve from another. What happens is that one dominant species dies out and is succeeded by a previously insignificant species. This second dominant species is descended from a not very remote ancestor common to both species. Every species that perishes is succeeded by its distant cousin. This principle seems to apply to institutions and social systems as much as to biological species.

In the Mesozoic period the air was occupied by pterodactyls—great flying reptiles with featherless, skinny wings. Today birds occupy the place in nature which pterodactyls

[1] L. P. Edwards, "Manufacturing Reds," *Atlantic Monthly*, July, 1920.

formerly held. But birds have not evolved from pterodactyls. The pterodactyls are all dead and have left no descend-
ants. The birds of today are descended from true, but primitive, Mesozoic birds, that in turn evolved from a small,
generalized reptile, which was the common ancestor of both
birds and pterodactyls.

Elephants and hippopotomi live today in areas of jungle
and swamp formerly occupied by the great dinosaurs. But
elephants and hippopotomi have not evolved from the great
dinosaurs. The great dinosaurs are all extinct. So are the
lesser ones, with a few, relatively unimportant, exceptions
such as alligators and crocodiles. When the dinosaurs
flourished the ancestors of our elephants and hippopotomi
were comparatively small, helpless creatures whose insignificance protected them from destruction by the dinosaurs.
The common ancestor of elephants, hippopotomi, and dinosaurs was a moderate-sized, primitively constructed
amphibian.

The principle illustrated in the foregoing cases can be
extended almost indefinitely. The "coal baron" and the
"steel king" occupy the same position of dominance in
present-day society that the feudal baron and king held in
the Middle Ages. But our present-day coal barons and steel
kings have not evolved from the feudal barons and kings,
though they happen to have the old titles applied to them
by popular usage. They have evolved from persons of the
lower classes in the Middle Ages, from persons much inferior
to the feudal barons and kings: Both the modern coal
baron and the old feudal baron, however, are in most cases
descended from those simple, rude barbarians who overthrew the Roman Empire. Some of them are Jews.

To go a step farther back. The feudal baron succeeded

to the place of the ancient Roman patrician. But the feudal
baron's ancestors were mere barbarians in the days when
the Roman patrician flourished. However, both the feudal
baron and the Roman patrician were descended from the
nomadic peoples who invaded Europe at the close of the
New Stone Age.

The control of present-day society is largely in the
hands of capitalists. But this control is being more and more
challenged, and even superseded, by labor-union control.
Fifty years ago, and less, the power of the capitalist was, to
a high degree, autocratic. Labor unions were few and feeble.
Today the power of the union is much more nearly on an
equality with that of the capitalist. Of the general trend of
affairs there can be no doubt. The power of capital, while
perhaps absolutely increasing, is relatively decreasing. The
power of labor seems to be increasing both absolutely and
relatively.

If the doctrines of the socialists are true, it may be predicted that a new social order will emerge—an order in
which the control of society will be transferred from prop-
erty-owners to "workers by hand and brain." A laboring
man of today—except, perhaps, in Russia—is a person still
insignificant compared to a capitalist. But through the
agency of his organization he is superior to the farmer. The
laboring man seems destined to be the ruler of the future.
The capitalist, very possibly, may become as extinct as the
feudal baron and the Roman patrician who preceded him.
The "labor baron" of the future will not evolve from the
coal baron of today. He will evolve from the labor leader
of today. Both he and the coal baron will have as a common ancestor the workingman of the not very distant past.

It is interesting and important to observe that when one

dominant species supplants another or when one human type is succeeded by another the change is not, ordinarily, the result of war and does not involve bloodshed. It is true that changes in human society are, at times, accompanied by wars and violence. But such outbreaks are, for the most part, mere symptoms. They are the visible evidence that changes have already taken place. The changes themselves are generally so gradual and peaceable as to be almost imperceptible.

It was not the wars of religion in the sixteenth century which overthrew the medieval papacy. That once powerful institution had been slowly disintegrated by a long series of previous events. The invention of printing, the rise of historical criticism, the growth of strong monarchies—all these and others like them had destroyed the real power of the medieval system before ever Luther nailed his theses to the door of the Wittenberg church. Except for these things, the opposition of the Protestants to the popes in the sixteenth century would have proved as vain as the opposition of the Albigenses proved in the thirteenth century. The religious wars of the sixteenth century did serve a purpose. They gave social sanction to Protestantism. But the overthrow of the medieval religious system was essentially accomplished before the religious wars began.

Similarly, the overthrow of the monarchy and feudal system in France was not caused by the French Revolution. The Revolution simply made evident the fact that the real power in France had passed into the hands of the middle class. It is plain that in the seventeenth century, and earlier, the power in France belonged to the king and the aristocracy. The real reasons why they lost it were the rise of large scale industrial and financial organizations, the great development of trade and commerce, the growth of a wealthy and intelligent middle class, the fashion of philosophizing about the foundations of government and law. Such things as these overthrew the old régime in France. The storming of the Bastille was merely a dramatic incident. Had it not been for the quiet and peaceful changes, Louis XVI probably could have suppressed the Revolution of 1789 as easily as Charles the Bad suppressed the Jacquerie of 1359.[1]

In a similar manner we can explain the fall of Russian czardom or the apparently impending succession of labor dominance to that of the capitalists in our own society. The desperate and often bloody conflicts between capital and labor are of no great historical significance in themselves. They merely make plain the fact that the control of modern society is passing from bankers and business men to coal miners and locomotive engineers. The miners and engineers can starve and freeze the rest of us. But this power has

[1] "The century and more of unrest which preceded both the Reformation and the French Revolution is in each instance a long story. But in both there was the same gradual loss of prestige on the part of the dominant crowd; the same inability of this crowd to change with the changes of time; to find new sanctions for itself when the old ones were no longer believed; the same unadaptability, the same intellectual and moral bankruptcy, therefore the same gradual disintegration from within; the same resort to sentimentalism and ineffective use of force, the same circle of hungry counter-crowds waiting around with their tongues hanging out, ready to pounce upon that before which they had previously groveled, and to justify their ravenousness as devotion to principle; the same growing fearlessness, beginning as perfectly loyal desire to reform certain abuses incidental to the existing order, and advancing, with every sign of disillusionment or weakness, to moral indignation, open attack upon fundamental control ideas, bitter hostility, augmented by the repressive measures taken by the dominant crowd to conserve a status quo which no longer gained assent in the minds of a growing counter-crowd; finally force, and a new dominant crowd more successful now in justifying old tyrannies by principles not yet successfully challenged."—Everett Dean Martin, *The Behavior of Crowds*, pp. 188–89.

come to them by quite peaceable means. It is due to the growth of large cities, the specialization of industry, the increased use of machinery, the development of railroads, and other causes which operate quite irrespective of strikes and lockouts.

The much-dreaded "social revolution," if it comes at all, will probably not be associated with violence. It will be caused by the sum total of peaceable changes and developments which have taken place since the last revolution. There need be no violence in it at all. There was almost none during the Industrial Revolution of the later eighteenth and early nineteenth centuries. Yet that was probably the greatest social revolution which has ever occurred on this planet. A real revolution is almost always a slow, essentially peaceable, and largely unnoticed process. The violent outbreaks commonly called revolutions are, in great measure, due to that conservatism which makes the economically favored classes unwilling to recognize the fact that a real and peaceable revolution has already occurred.

Since the Mesozoic pterodactyls were so large and powerful and the birds of that period so small and feeble, how did it come about that the pterodactyls perished while the birds survived? Similarly, why did the relatively small ancestors of the elephant and hippopotomus supersede the huge and terrible dinosaurs of the ancient time?

As before stated, it was not primarily by strife and bloodshed. The truth seems to be that every organism tends to create conditions which ultimately destroy it. One way this takes place is by size. Shortly before any dominant species of man or animal, of institution or civilization, becomes extinct, it grows and develops so greatly that it gets out of harmony with its surroundings. It cannot obtain the increased nourishment or support its excessive bulk requires. So it perishes and its place is taken by some smaller, but more active and economical, cousin species or organization. It would seem that Nature, having determined to destroy a species, allows it to flower gloriously just before its end.

The trilobites, those most famous of ancient mollusks, were of moderate size through most of their long history. Shortly before they became extinct they developed enormously. Some of them had shells three or four feet in diameter. Just why they perished, nobody knows for certain, but all the evidence seems to show that they kept on getting larger and larger, long after that had ceased to be an advisable thing for them to do. Exactly the same is true of the pterodactyls. Some of these creatures attained a wing spread of more than twenty feet, shortly before the extinction of the species. The dinosaurs have an identical history. For a while, just before they perished, they grew to an almost incredible size—some of them were eighty or even one hundred feet in length. They were the largest land animals that ever existed. But they became too large and clumsy for their environment. So they too became extinct, giving way to smaller, but more active and intelligent animals.

The excess-development theory would seem to apply even to inanimate things. A stick of common blackboard chalk, a half-inch thick and six inches long, coheres very well. Increase its length to twelve inches and it will break under a very small fraction of the strain which the six-inch stick can bear easily. The longer it is, the more easily it will break. It will have reached its greatest length just before it breaks under its own weight.

The same thing is true of institutions. The medieval

church flowered out into the most luxurious richness of cathedrals, abbeys, statues, pictures, painted glass, and every form of expensive beauty and ornament just before the Reformation. The extravagant luxury and profuseness of the old régime in France culminated very shortly before the Revolution.

The enormous bulk and pretentious equipment of ocean passenger steamers would seem indicative of excess development. They are getting too large for all but a few harbors. The cost of running them is disproportionately great. The smaller, swifter, and more economical aeroplane is rapidly developing. It is not improbable that, in the not distant future, the ocean passenger steamer will be displaced, just as it, in days gone by, displaced the sailing ship.

The huge size and enormous wealth of the trusts and syndicates of the present day would seem to indicate that they have entered their period of excess development. They will, very possibly, become larger and wealthier than they are now. But they already exhibit symptoms of being out of harmony with their environment. They seem destined to perish before some more suitable form of industrial organization—perhaps the lowly, co-operative enterprise.

The excess-development theory has a bearing on the question of war. The size, the ferocity, the destructiveness, and expensiveness of civilized warfare have increased progressively for several centuries. We are not far wrong, perhaps, in the opinion that war, too, has entered its period of excess development. Judging by the late conflict, war cannot become much more deadly without putting an end to itself by destroying the "civilized" nations that indulge in it. There is the alternative possibility that war may become extinct by the growth of the, at present, feeble movement for settling international disputes by arbitration and judicial procedure. This is, as yet, only a possibility. It is a very remote possibility, as long as nationalistic patriotism flourishes in its present luxuriance. Our present-day nationalities are in themselves the successors to the empires that flourished during a preceding period of empire-building. The decomposition of the vast world-empires into nationalities is still going on.

In the long run, it is the "common sense" of the ordinary man which decides the fate of all institutions. In this case common sense is gradually coming over to the support of a better system. Civilized men are today divided into a large number of politically independent groups. Each such independent nation possesses the "right" to make war—the right to commit murder, robbery, and arson at will and by wholesale. Such an arrangement is as contrary to common sense as it is to ethics. A growth of common sense or a religious revival, carrying with it an ethical advance, may ultimately put an end to the sovereignty of nations as it exists today. Nations are essentially fighting organizations. They all originated in war, and it is very possible they will all perish in war.

It would appear that mankind has made a false start—run into a blind alley—in the matter of nationalistic patriotism. There is nothing to be ashamed of in this. So far as we can see, the whole course of evolution is a process of trial and error. Nature, it seems, makes many false starts and goes up innumerable blind alleys. Take the matter of animal development: Millions of years ago she tried her hand with the mollusks and developed the great trilobites whose shells adorn our natural-history museums. This attempt to make a high-type animal failed, and Nature put an end to the trilobites by means of excess development. Un-discouraged, she tried again and again and again with fish and amphibians and reptiles and mammals, until at last she attained a measure of success in the case of man. Even here she had several failures at first. Pithecanthropus, Eoanthropos, and several other types of early man did not "make good" and became extinct.

It is the same story in social organization. The horde, the tribe, the military monarchy, and the feudal system have all been tried repeatedly. All have flourished for their little day, but all have been mere figures in the long procession of history. National democracy is not the final form of social organization. It is only one of a continuous series of forms. The next form in the series would appear to be some sort of world-society ethically and economically superior to independent nationalism. Some sort of world-society will surely come. When it does come, it will relegate war to that museum of ancient horrors where cannibalism and slavery have already found their place.[1]

Most of what has been said about war applies with equal or greater force to violent revolution. In present-day civilization a violent revolution of a thoroughgoing sort involves such destruction as to threaten the existence of the society involved. There is increasing evidence that the Russian Revolution will result very much as the French Revolution did, in the triumph of the bourgeoisie. Yet the twentieth-century Russian Revolution was much more destructive than the eighteenth-century French Revolution. Similarly, the eighteenth-century French Revolution was much more destructive than the seventeenth-century English Revolu-

[1] See the discussion of this subject in Graham Wallas, *Human Nature in Politics*, and particularly in the chapter, "Nationality and Humanity."

tion. This increasing destructiveness of violent revolution from the seventeenth-century to the twentieth seems to be due, in part, to the fact that the repression of elemental wishes was more extensive in France than in England, and in Russia than in France. Largely, however, this increased destructiveness is to be ascribed to the increasing complexity of Western civilization from the seventeenth century onward. This complexity, it is perhaps needless to say, is increasing daily. War is now much more destructive than it was formerly, and a thoroughgoing violent revolution almost always involves civil war and generally foreign wars as well. A technique for obviating this kind of social upheaval is as much a necessity for the survival of Western civilization as is a technique for the abolition of the war system. The will to do away with war is already here.

SELECTED REFERENCES

ADAMS, BROOKS. *The Theory of Social Revolutions.* New York, 1913.

BAUER, ARTHUR, *Essai sur les révolutions.* Paris, 1908.

EDWARDS, L. P. "Manufacturing Reds," *Atlantic Monthly*, July, 1920.

ELLWOOD, CHARLES A. "A Psychological Study of Revolutions," *American Journal of Sociology*, XI (1905), 49–59.

LIMAN, PAUL. *Die Revolution: Eine vergleichende Studie über die grossen Umwälzungen in der Geschichte.* Berlin, 1906.

MARTIN, EVERETT DEAN. *The Behavior of Crowds; a Psychological Study.* New York and London, 1920.

OGBURN, WILLIAM F. *Social Change.* New York, 1922.

PARK, R. E., AND BURGESS, E. W. *Introduction to the Science of Sociology*, chaps. vii and xiii (Bibliography), Chicago, 1923.

POSTGATE, RAYMOND WILLIAM (ed.). *Revolution from 1789 to 1906; Documents Selected and Edited with Notes and Introductions.* London, 1920.

SOROKIN, PITIRIM A. *The Sociology of Revolution.* Philadelphia and London, 1925.

WALLACE, ALFRED RUSSEL. *The World of Life. A Manifestation of Creative Power, Directive Mind, and Ultimate Purpose*, chap. xiii. New York, 1911.

WALLAS, GRAHAM. *Human Nature in Politics*. London, 1908.

YODER, DALE. "Current Definitions of Revolution," *American Journal of Sociology*, XXXII (1926), 433–41.

CHAPTER II

THE SLOW DEVELOPMENT OF REVOLUTIONARY MOVEMENTS

There is a popular opinion that revolutions are sudden, unpredictable, and exceedingly rapid in their development. This opinion is mistaken. It is even ludicrously mistaken. A revolution, in certain respects, resembles an elephant. The elephant is the slowest breeding of all living creatures, and a revolution is the slowest forming of all social movements. There is not, so far as the writer is aware, a real revolution in all human history which developed in less than three generations. Of course the so-called revolutions which so persistently afflict the Balkan States and the South American republics are not revolutions in this meaning of the word.[1] The Balkan and South American "revolutions" are mere outbreaks of lawlessness which leave the institutions of the countries concerned practically unchanged. They mean no more than elections in more stable societies. And elections are themselves mere substitutes for civil war. It seems, on the whole, more profitable, even if less interesting, to count noses rather than break heads.

[1] Ellwood has pointed out that when a revolutionary party is united in nothing except in its opposition to the old régime, and when the abuses and immobility of the old order have left the mass of the population ignorant, degraded, and without the power of intelligent adaptation, the period of confusion, anarchy, and mob rule incident to the attempted change may continue for a long time. This condition, not infrequently illustrated by some Central and some South American countries, he has designated as "a state of chronic revolution."—Charles A. Ellwood, *The Psychology of Human Society*, p. 260.

The reason why it takes at least three generations to develop a revolution is simple. When a given social institution begins to function badly the generation then alive, the first generation to suffer, can remember it when it functioned well and believe that it can be restored to useful activity by means of some minor reforms. This belief proves erroneous, but the second generation are brought up to hold it, and in any case they have heard the first generation tell personal experiences of the former successful functioning of the detrimental institution. So the second generation still love and venerate it, in spite of its increasing social inadequacy. The third generation experience continually greater frustration of their elemental wishes as the institution becomes more and more archaic. Since they find nobody who has had personal experience of its successful functioning, the harmful institution is sometimes destroyed by the third generation of those it harms. This, however, is very rare. Generally the third generation still have a strong attachment to the old institution, an attachment in part derived from tales of its former excellence, heard in early youth from grandparents and other elderly persons. In the great majority of cases it is in the fourth generation, or later, that the overthrow of the old institution occurs.

One or two historical illustrations may help to make this point clear. The Bourbon monarchy in France first revealed serious incapacity in the later part of the seventeenth century. The expulsion of the Huguenots, the ruinous wars, the heavy taxation, the inequitable incidence of taxation, the enormous expense of the luxurious and extravagant court—these factors created widespread discontent in France at least a century before the meeting of the States General. If revolutions were as sudden as they are sometimes supposed to be, the French Revolution would have taken place in 1689 instead of 1789. As a matter of fact, though the French people suffered from misgovernment in 1689 they were devotedly attached to the monarchy at that time and for more than a hundred years after—in spite of the fact that their monarchy became progressively more inefficient. In 1689 there was discontent with the government of Louis XIV, but the people of that generation could remember an earlier period of his reign which stands in history forever as one of the "great ages" of France. They had grievances against the monarchy, but for the most part their experience with it had been satisfactory—an experience, indeed, of which they were with justice immensely proud. In spite of their grievances, nobody in that generation had the remotest thought of abolishing the monarchy. All they asked was reduction of taxation and some minor administrative reforms.

The next generation, who were in charge of things about 1720, could not themselves remember the monarchy as either great or beneficent. But as children they had heard their parents and grandparents tell of the glorious days of the preceding century. They gained in childhood, and retained through life, a strong attachment to the monarchy, though their own experience of it was consistently unsatisfactory. Their faith and loyalty may be judged by the fact that Louis XV was, to them, Louis "the Well Beloved."

The third generation, of 1750, were not so naïve in their attachment to the monarchy as their fathers had been. The glories of the previous century were mere history to them, while the evils they suffered from their corrupt government were real and immediate. So they raised questions about the theory of government. The encyclopedists belonged to this generation. Yet such was the power of habituation, such was the influence of tradition, so hard was it to entertain the thought of doing away with an old and thoroughly established institution, that even in 1750 not 1 per cent of the French people had any serious idea of abolishing the monarchy.

The fourth generation did, indeed, replace the monarchy by a republic. Yet when the republic was set up in 1793, its establishment was far more the result of external circumstances than of any previously determined purpose on the part of the mass of the people. Old, blind, crazy, and hopeless as their monarchy was, the French gave it up reluctantly and only under the pressure of the most imperious necessity.

The slowness of development which we have noted in the French Revolution will be found upon investigation to be characteristic of any great social upheaval. That important religious revolution called the Protestant Reformation is an example. It is no great exaggeration to say that, for more than two hundred years before the Reformation, the history of the papacy was one long scandal. The Babylonian captivity; the Great Schism, with two popes, and sometimes three, mutually cursing one another; the corruption and immorality of the most highly placed clergymen—all these things are so well known that it is unnecessary to dwell upon them. Yet this scandalous condition of affairs lasted for a hundred years before there was any real effort to establish a purer form of religious institutions. Two attempts were then made: that of Wickliffe in England and that of Huss in Bohemia. Both Wickliffe and Huss were men of eminent virtue and ability. Yet they both failed. The chief reason for their failure was the loyalty of the people of

Western Europe to their traditional ecclesiastical system. That loyalty was still strong after they had experienced for a century the papacy's vice and corruption. Another century of still greater vice and corruption was necessary in order to develop sufficient discontent to make a successful religious revolution possible.

There is hardly anything more pathetic in the history of the human mind than the moral agony of devout and pious Europeans of the fourteenth and fifteenth centuries. For seven successive generations godly and religious men and women somehow managed to retain their faith in the papacy in spite of their horror of its wickedness. Age after age they labored and prayed in anguish of spirit for its purification. After more than two hundred years of vain effort at reformation, a generation came which abandoned the ancient faith. But they did so with the greatest sorrow and heaviness of heart. It is noteworthy that even after it had alienated the allegiance and aroused the antagonism of great and powerful nations, even in the very floodtide of the Protestant movement, the ancient church was able to save herself from destruction and to retain the loyalty of tens of millions of people by a very moderate amount of internal renovation, which probably did not raise the curia to any higher level of virtue than a body of Christian ministers might reasonably be expected to possess.

It would only labor the point to give further historical illustrations of the slowness of revolutions in coming to a head. The English Revolution, the American Revolution, the Russian Revolution—all show this characteristic of slow development. Perhaps because it values them more highly, society changes its religious institutions even more slowly than it does the others. It took more than three hundred

years for so pure a religion as early Christianity to overthrow so degenerate a religion as Roman paganism.

Any institution, no matter how foolish or pernicious, if
only it is firmly fixed in the mores, will continue to exist in
spite of the clearest demonstration of its harmfulness, until
sheer necessity forces its abolition. Man is largely a crea-
ture of habit and tradition. Most of his institutions are the
products of sentiment, not of reason. He will endure great
suffering and loss rather than drop from his social order any
institution to which he has been long accustomed. It means
nothing that an alternative institution is offered him. The
new institution may be greatly superior to the old, but it
is not the old, and so it will be admitted only grudgingly and
under the pressure of urgent necessity.

Of the social institutions existing at any given time in
any given civilization, a large number are archaic and a still
larger number are by way of becoming so. Only in Western
Europe and its colonies is there any popular idea of progress.
Even where the idea exists, it generally is confined to tech-
nical inventions. Very rarely does it embrace social and political institutions.[1] A contemporary American desires to
have an automobile of the model of the current year, but he
is quite fanatically attached to a political machine of the
model of 1787. *The Origin of Species* was published in 1859,
but millions of people are still defending the Book of
Genesis against Darwin. More than a century of anti-saloon
agitation preceded the adoption of the prohibition amendment. Yet the amendment seems a failure because public
opinion was not sufficiently prepared for it.

[1] For a sociological discussion of the theories of progress and the place
of progress in social evolution see Ferdinand Tönnies, "Fortschritt und
Soziale Entwicklung," *Jahrbuch für Soziologie*, I (1925), 166–221.

SELECTED REFERENCES

CREIGHTON, MANDELL. *History of the Papacy during the Period of the Reformation*, Vol. I. London, 1887–94.

EDWARDS, LYFORD P. "The Mechanics of Revolution," *St. Stephen's College Bulletin*, Vol. LXIV, No. 2.

ELLWOOD, CHARLES A. *The Psychology of Human Society*. New York and London, 1925.

GEIGER, THEODORE. *Die Masse und Ihre Aktion: Ein Beitrag zur Soziologie der Revolutionen*. Stuttgart, 1926.

KAUTSKY, KARL. *Foundations of Christianity*. New York, 1925.

KITCHIN, GEORGE WILLIAMS. *A History of France* (3d ed.), Vol. III, Books V and VI. Oxford, 1892–96.

TÖNNIES, FERDINAND. "Rechtlinien für das Studium des Fortschritts und der sozialen Entwicklung," *Jahrbuch für Soziologie*, I (1925), 166–221.

TOYNBEE, ARNOLD. *Lectures on the Industrial Revolution of the Eighteenth Century in England*. London, 1908.

CHAPTER III

PRELIMINARY SYMPTOMS OF UNREST

The earliest symptom of a coming revolution is an increase of general restlessness. A certain amount of restlessness is normal and socially healthy. There is no method of quantitative measurement by which it is possible to determine just how much restlessness indicates a pathological social condition. With the progress of time, any established social order tends to become stiff and rigid. Its institutions ossify. The elemental human wishes for new experience, security, recognition, and response are thwarted. Opportunities for their realization become less and general restlessness results. But for a long time the situation is not understood. The feeling of restlessness is at first very vague and indefinite. Nobody makes any effort to study it or to find out the causes of it. All the effort is in the direction of satisfying it by mere movement or purposeless activity. There is an increase of travel, for the relationship between travel and social unrest is reciprocal. Unrest increases travel and travel increases unrest.

The provincial often returns from his trip abroad with a heightened attachment to his own habitat, but this is not always the case. A New Yorker who has visited Wiesbaden becomes critical of Saratoga Springs. A German who has seen New York City at night expresses discontent at the evening gloominess of Berlin. An American Congressman, after attending "question hour" in the House of Commons, begins to entertain doubts about the constitutional separation of the executive and legislative departments of his own government. An Englishman, after experience with the social equality in America, loses some of his reverence for the House of Lords. The institutions of one's society look different at a distance and in the midst of another people. Comparisons in such a situation are inevitable and not all of them are favorable to the home society. Very loyal Americans assert that there is no beverage in the United States so good as the beer in Munich.

A pronounced influence in this respect is exercised by strangers entering provincial groups. It is a matter of common knowledge that in every social upheaval the party attacked claims that the trouble has been stirred up by outside agents and agitators. This claim, made throughout history, contains a certain element of truth. The "outsider" is not bound by the peculiar traditions, prejudices, customs, pieties, and precedents of the group he enters.[1] He views that group in a less sentimental and more rational manner. He sees its institutions in a more objective light. He judges them more intelligently as well as more critically, and he is not always silent or discreet. He points out maladjustments and deficiencies. He opens the eyes of the people to their own shortcomings. He institutes comparisons between that group and other more advanced groups with which he is familiar.

There are, however, limitations to the "outsider's" influence. There is initial prejudice against him as an "outsider." His social contacts are incomplete. He rarely, or never, succeeds in stirring up agitation unless the conditions are such as to justify discontent. If the discontent already exists the "outsider" can bring it to light. This is a useful

[1] See Georg Simmel, *Soziologie*, pp. 509–12.

public service, not often recognized as such. But neither the "outsider" nor the "insider" can stir up discontent unless the discontent is there to be stirred up. An "outsider" is not so good an agitator as an "insider" who returns to the community after having been for some time in a more advanced society. Those Indian Brahmins are indeed wise who forbid all foreign travel as dangerous to the caste system.

At the preliminary stage of affairs we are now considering, it is probable that nobody has the remotest notion of any revolution—not even the travelers themselves. They do not realize why they travel. Indeed, much of the travel is mere idle and aimless wandering. Luther's journey to Rome is important in the preparation for the Reformation but nobody knew it at the time—least of all Luther. The early Christians wandering through the Roman Empire had no idea of the tremendous results that were to come from their missionary journeys. As a matter of fact, those results were not generally perceived until centuries after the twelve apostles were in their graves. The wandering university students of the thirteenth and fourteenth centuries broke the road for the Renaissance, but they never knew they were doing it. Of the countless thousands of knights and barons who went on the Crusades few or none perceived how those military wanderings were to aid in overthrowing the feudal system. The inveterate peripatetic habits of the Greek and Roman philosophers, more especially in the two or three generations preceding the overthrow of the Roman Republic, are well known. The ancient classical philosophers seem always to have had the wanderlust. But the evidence appears fairly conclusive that this perambulatory bent was markedly accentuated during the period between the Roman conquest of Greece and the establishment of the Roman Empire.

The French philosophers of the first three quarters of the eighteenth century hold a record for peregrination. Voltaire's travels had a marked influence on the development of French political thinking in the period preceding the Revolution. The other philosophers were not much behind Voltaire; Rousseau's *Confessions* were written in England.

Russians were notable for their traveling propensities a full century before the Revolution of 1917. The present government of Russia is composed of men who have traveled or wandered over nearly every country on earth. Less than a year before he became dictator, Lenin was living in Switzerland. At that same time Trotsky's address was the Bronx. More than a half-century earlier, the wanderings of two revolutionary aristocrats, Bakunin and Kropotkin, advertised to all Europe the repressive despotism of the czars.

Another illustration is that of the Hebrew race. Throughout all their long and wonderful history, the Jews have been the most foot-loose as well as the most revolutionary people on record. The noblest succession of revolutionists that ever lived, those prophets whose writings make up so large a part of the Bible, were many of them exiles and all of them influenced by the Seventy Years Exile of their race. With all reverence, a still more sacred example may be cited. The world's greatest revolutionist, whom hundreds of millions of men worship as God, was a wanderer who had not where to lay his head.

Continuing the ancient tradition of Moses and the prophets, the greatest of modern revolutionists, Karl Marx, "the Father of Socialism," was a Jew who spent his life in exile, driven continually from one country to another.

To conclude this point with a reference to the history of the United States, it is notable that the Jews were conspicuous for their support of the cause of independence while a great part of Washington's army was made up of exiled Irishmen and of frontiersmen, those restless pioneers to whom the very thought of a settled life and a permanent abode was intolerable.

It is not contended that a mere increase of travel by itself portends revolution. Travel may obviously increase greatly from causes quite unconnected with the repression of elemental wishes. All that is claimed is that an increase of travel does characterize any society in which a revolutionary movement is coming into being.

The restlessness of such a society finds expression chiefly among the upper and middle classes, through travel of a more or less conventional kind. The lower strata of society are effected in a corresponding but slightly different manner. There is an increase of hobos, tramps, and bums. A hobo may be defined as a migratory worker, while a tramp is a migratory non-worker, and a bum is a non-migratory non-worker. Under various names—"sturdy beggars," "idle vagabonds," "lazy rogues"—these three classes increase in any society during the period preceding a great revolution. They constitute a considerable part of the "raw material" from which revolutionary mobs are formed. The early stages of elemental wish repression produce a mere indefinite feeling of uneasiness in the upper classes. The effect on the lower orders is more marked. Landless peasants are driven into the big cities—whether ancient Rome or modern Moscow. They do not or cannot find work at "a living wage." Charity, no matter how extensive, does not mend matters much. There is an increase in crime, especially passionate crime. Vice, insanity, divorce, and suicide assume proportions that alarm all the moralists. These evils are not long confined to the lower orders. They become equally common and more conspicuous among the upper classes. Through the whole of society they are to be understood as "compensation devices"—perversions which develop because the normal methods of wish fulfilment are blocked. Wickedness is only human energy which does not find a healthy outlet.

Here again a caveat must be entered. Vice, crime, poverty, and similar evils have existed in every civilization. They may increase to very startling proportions without presaging a revolution. In spite of popular opinion to the contrary, it is doubtful whether such evils have ever been a real menace to any well-established social order. It is certain that they have never, of themselves, succeeded in destroying any civilization. Waves of criminality and viciousness appear and disappear at various times and for many different reasons. They are characteristic of young and vigorous societies as well as of old and feeble ones; that is to say, they appear after a revolution as well as before it. All of this does not affect the argument. Wherever or whenever else it may appear, a conspicuous degree of immorality does show itself in any society in which a great revolutionary upheaval is in process of development. It commonly makes its first appearance somewhat later than does the traveling previously noted, but for a considerable period the two symptoms of unrest are concurrent. Both are commonly discoverable before any more specific evidences of social disorganization become visible.

Historical examples of the immorality of pre-revolutionary societies are both numerous and well known. Fortunately, it is not necessary to dwell upon them at length. The licentiousness, the baseness, the cruelty, the extravagance, the corruption, the selfishness, and the frivolity of the curia and of many lower clergy of the pre-Reformation Catholic church make one of the most shameful chapters in the history of Christianity.

A similar period of disgrace, the details of which may be spared, marked French society for a long period before the Revolution. The fathomless corruption, both of the aristocracy and the proletariat of Rome in the last century of the republic, stands pilloried forever in the pages of Sallust and Cicero.

Three generations of great Russian authors have described the society of their country during the past seventy-five years. They have described that society in all its aspects, with the most careful accuracy and with the highest literary skill. The impression they make upon their readers is so painful that the morbidity of Russian literature is a byword. Yet the morbidity is only in the literature because it was in the society which the literature depicts.

In English history the dissoluteness of the Restoration has somewhat obscured that of the reign of James I. Yet in the reign of James I, Francis Bacon, the philosopher, confessed to twenty-eight charges of bribery while holding the highest judicial position in England, and a reading of the trial of the Earl of Somerset for poisoning Sir Thomas Overbury[1] reveals a widespread condition of moral rottenness which can only be described as pathological. The court of Charles I, like that of Louis XVI, was somewhat better than the preceding one in point of private conduct, but its sinecures, its pensions, and its extravagance are notorious.

[1] *State Trials*, I, 230 ff.

Puritanism developed, in part at least, as a reaction against the prevailing immorality of the times.

Coming to American history, a decent regard for the conventionalities of contemporary patriotism forbids any imputation of peccability to the "Heroes of 1776." Similarly, the earlier generations of colonists have a halo of sanctity which it would be highly indecorous to disturb. Nevertheless, some "disloyal and un-American" historians, learned in the life of those times, report things which might, perhaps, be perverted into a claim that the Thirteen Colonies were not totally lacking in certain unsavory phenomena characteristic of other societies in the periods preceding their revolutions. Be it admitted, in all justice, that these phenomena were not of so outstanding a character in America as in many other places.

A third preliminary symptom of revolution is the establishment of a definite mental attitude—that known as the "balked disposition." People come to feel that their legitimate aspirations and ideals are being repressed or perverted, that their entirely proper desires and ambitions are being hindered and thwarted—they do not know how or why. Disappointment and discouragement become widespread. Work becomes unsatisfactory and monotonous to great numbers of people. Life itself becomes stale and objectless. Throughout society there runs a strong, though inarticulate, demand for new stimulation and fresh incentives. The unrest which has been previously unconscious or subconscious becomes in a measure objectified. People gradually realize that "there is something rotten in the state of Denmark." Still the degree of objectification is slight. The dominant characteristic is mere discontent with the established routine of life—but this discontent begins to be contagious.

"Unrest in the individual becomes social. It is, or seems to be transmitted from one individual to another, so that the manifestations of discontent in A communicated to B, and from B reflected back to A, produce a circular reaction."[1] It is a "vicious circle." Every expression of discontent aggravates the discontent. The process is of a very elemental, even instinctive, sort. Psychologically, it is similar to the behavior of some of the lower animals.

Under the influence of a vague sense of alarm, or merely as an effect of heat or thirst, cattle become restless and begin slowly moving about in circles, "milling." This milling is a sort of collective gesture, an expression of discontent and of fear. Milling in the herd is a visible image of what goes on in subtle and less obvious ways in human societies.[2]

After repression of elemental wishes has continued for some considerable period in any human society, a condition of *rapport* is gradually established among the individuals suffering the repression. "*Rapport* implies the existence of a mutual responsiveness, such that every member of the group reacts immediately, spontaneously and sympathetically to the sentiments and attitudes of every other member." Such *rapport* is a thing of very slow growth in any large social group. "The fact that A responds sympathetically to B and C implies the existence in A of an attitude of receptivity and suggestibility towards the sentiments and attitudes of B and C."[3] But such a condition comes about only after A, B, and C have been subjected for a considerable time to similar experiences. The degree in which we respond to a suggestion is conditioned upon its

[1] Park and Burgess, *Introduction to the Science of Sociology*, p. 866.
[2] *Ibid.*, p. 893.
[3] *Ibid.*

relation to our past experience. We respond to our own idea of the suggestion, and not to the idea as conceived by the person making it.

In a repressed society small local groups casually meeting together become sympathetic through their mutual experience of repression. "The inhibitions which under ordinary circumstances serve to preserve the isolation and self-consciousness of the individuals are relaxed or completely broken down." But the process, be it repeated, is a very gradual one. There is only the most elementary sort of collective behavior. There is discontent. There is the mutual expression of discontent. There is sympathy. There is the heightening of discontent through mutual expression and sympathy. But that is all. It is hardly more than the "milling" of a herd of cattle. There is no rational effort to get at the causes of discontent. There is no idea of organization to effect a remedy. There is no thought of revolution.

Life being thus restless and fretful and the cause of the condition not being understood, the more bold and active members of the group seek release through emigration. A large part of Gaul was settled by Roman emigrants of this type in the first century B.C. The "Mayflower" and many another ship brought emigrants of the same type to America. The French colony of Canada had numbers of them. Even in the Colonial period of American history, men discontented with the restraints of life in the seaboard colonies went pioneering into the western wilderness.

But it is easy to exaggerate this. Purely economic forces regularly cause emigration from a region of smaller natural resources to one of greater. Emigration from Italy to America would take place even if the social order in Italy were as perfect as any social order can be conceived to be.

When a great social revolution is to eventuate in any society, no large proportion of its bold and daring members emigrate from that society. Not all the Puritans came to New England. Most of them stayed in old England, dethroned the king, and cut off his head. In spite of local opinion to the contrary, New York City does not contain all the Russian Jews in the world. Most of them remained in Russia where they took a conspicuous part in the Revolution.

Nevertheless, emigration from a given society is, in certain cases, a sign of "balked disposition" due to social repression in that society and in such cases is a precursor of revolution. The circumstances of the emigration must be examined with great care. In itself, emigration is a preventive of revolution. Oliver Cromwell desired to get away from England and to settle in Massachusetts. He was stopped at the dock by officers of Charles I. Had he been allowed to leave the country, it is conceivable that Charles I might have di~d of old age.

The difficulty of analyzing its causes deprives emigration of much of its diagnostic value as a preliminary symptom of revolution. Yet, in some measure, it has such value, and with due precaution should be taken into account.

The next preliminary symptom to be noted is a marked increase of wealth, intelligence, and power in the repressed portion of society. This phenomenon does not accord with popular opinion. But it is an invariable and essential step in pre-revolutionary development. There is a common belief that a great revolution is preceded by the ever increasing misery and oppression of the people. The legend has it that the repressed classes suffer continually greater and greater poverty and hunger, tyranny and misrule, until human nature can stand no more. It would be an exaggeration to say that this legend is the exact reverse of the facts. But the exaggeration would not be excessive. The repression of elemental wishes during any pre-revolutionary period is not greater than in earlier generations of the same society. Very generally the amount of repression is less. But even though actually smaller, it seems larger and creates greater discontent. The reason for this is simple. Through the ordinary progress of civilization, by improvements and inventions and discoveries of all sorts, the skill, the knowledge, the productivity, and the wealth of the lower class of people gradually increases. With this gradual increase of their wealth and knowledge comes a corresponding change in their beliefs and opinions, their sentiments and feelings. Conditions of life which were previously tolerable become intolerable; institutions formerly cherished are despised. Customs and ceremonies once revered are derided. The whole philosophy of life, earlier held to be virtuous or ever sacred, becomes pernicious or absurd.

But this change in mental attitude is subsequent to, and dependent upon, economic and cultural improvement. An increase of wealth in the repressed classes is observable some time before any marked change in their beliefs and sentiments can be detected. But that change always makes its appearance after a while, and always, at first, in the form of discontent. Just in proportion as the lower classes of the people become better off, they demand more social recognition, more freedom, more prestige, more control over the government, over the law courts, over the church, over all the institutions of social control. As they become more intelligent, they become more critical; and when conditions are not remedied, criticism passes into revolt. A smaller degree of repression is felt as more intolerable when one is "coming up in the world." People "on the make" are especially sensitive to any discrimination against themselves. So it often comes about that revolutions overthrow repressive institutions at the very time that those institutions are milder and less repressive than ever before. Similarly, people become most revolutionary and most resistant of oppression when the actual degree of oppression is least. That is to be expected, because under those conditions the people are best able to revolt and there is the most likelihood that a revolution will be successful. The emotion which furnishes the driving power to revolution is hope, not despair.

A few examples from history will help to make these points clear. The papacy of the early sixteenth century was undoubtedly very evil, but it shines with the halo of virtue and sanctity when compared to the papacy of the early tenth century. Pope Leo X, whatever his faults, was an angel of light compared to Pope John XI. Yet the religious revolution broke out in the pontificate of Leo X, not that of John XI. Charles I of England was unquestionably an arbitrary and tyrannical king, but he was a mild and constitutional monarch compared to Henry VIII. It is quite beyond dispute that the people of England were both more free and more prosperous under Charles I and James II than under Henry VIII and Elizabeth. Charles I and James II lost their crowns. Henry VIII and Elizabeth enjoyed enormous popularity.

The government of Louis XVI, at its worst, was immeasurably better than the government of Louis IX. Louis XVI went to the guillotine; Louis IX is in the calendar of saints. The French peasants who burned their lords alive in the "chateaux bonfires" of 1789 were the wealthiest, the most intelligent, and the least-oppressed peasants in Continental Europe—popular superstition to the contrary notwithstanding. The peasants of Hungary or Poland, who really were oppressed, ignorant, and poor, had not even a thought of revolution.

The American colonies that revolted against the misgovernment of George III were the freest and best-governed colonies in the world. They were better governed under George III than they had ever been under any previous king. The colonists who declared their independence in 1776 were in every respect better off than the colonists of 1700 who were enthusiastically loyal.

The czardom under Nicholas II, however repressive and reactionary, was humane and progressive compared to the czardom under Ivan the Terrible. Nicholas II was deposed and murdered. Ivan the Terrible lived to a ripe age in the full possession of absolute power. One of the noblest poems in Russian literature is a lament for his death.

The explanation in all these cases is the same: Revolutions do not occur when the repressed classes are forced down to the depths of misery.[1] Revolutions occur after the repressed classes, for a considerable time, have been in the enjoyment of increasing prosperity. A marked increase of power, intelligence, and wealth in the repressed portion of society is a phenomenon invariably found in the period preceding any great revolution. It is one of the most important symptoms of future upheaval.

[1] For a discussion of the negligible rôle played by the lowest economic class, "the Lumpenproletariat," see Karl Marx and Friedrich Engels, *The Communist Manifesto*.

SELECTED REFERENCES

FREIMARK, HANS. *Die Revolution als psychische Massenerscheinung.* Munich, 1920.

LE BON, GUSTAVE. *The Psychology of Peoples.* London, 1898.

MARX, KARL, AND ENGELS, FRIEDERICH. *The Communist Manifesto* (2d ed). London, 1888.

PARK, ROBERT E., AND BURGESS, ERNEST W. *Introduction to the Science of Sociology,* chap. xiii, "Collective Behavior." Chicago, 1923.

SIMMEL, GEORG. *Sociologie: Untersuchungen über die Formen der Gesellschaftung.* Munich and Leipzig, 1922.

State Trials for High Treason, I, 230 ff. London, 1794.

CHAPTER IV

ADVANCED SYMPTOMS OF REVOLUTION

All of the preliminary symptoms of revolution described in the preceding chapter are premonitory only. They occur before revolution but their occurrence does not mean that revolution necessarily follows. All of them are to be found, for instance, in England during the period preceding the Reform Bill of 1832. Yet the Reform Bill came in time to prevent revolution.

There now come up for consideration those more important phenomena which never occur unless a revolution does follow. There are a considerable number of these advanced symptoms of revolution, but they are all more or less dependent upon two master-symptoms—symptoms which, once clearly recognized, enable the social diagnostician to predict with a great degree of assurance the certainty of coming upheaval.

The first master-symptom of revolution is the "transfer of the allegiance of the intellectuals." The authors, the editors, the lecturers, the artists, the teachers, the priests, the preachers, and all those whose function it is to form and guide public opinion become infected with the discontent of the repressed classes of society. In order to appreciate the great importance of this intellectualist change of feeling it is necessary to recall the social function of the intellectuals.

All societies above the lower stages of barbarism have been composed of three classes of people: exploiters, non-productive laborers, and productive laborers. Exploiters are those who control, direct, and live by the labor of others, "without giving," as the revolutionists claim, "any equivalent labor in return." Productive laborers are those who do the work necessary to maintain society at the given level of culture. The non-productive laborers (the intellectuals) are the intermediate class whose work consists very largely in maintaining and transmitting the system intact to future generations.

The exploiters are relatively few in number but they control a great part, generally the greater part, of the capital and labor of society. Their essential characteristic is that they constitute, with the intellectuals, the "overhead," and so become a charge upon the producers in any society in which they exist.

The intellectuals are about as numerous as the exploiters—that is, they form only a small percentage of society. They own little, and live mostly by wages received from the exploiters. Their essential function is the creation and maintenance of the institution of "ownership" by which the exploiters live. The productive laborers form the vast majority of any society. Most of them own little or nothing. They, like the intellectuals, live on wages paid them by the exploiters.

These three classes have been known in the vocabulary of revolutionists by a great variety of names at different periods of history. Today exploiters are called "absentee owners," "capitalists," or "the bourgeoisie." Productive laborers are known as "workingmen," "wage slaves," or "the proletariat." Non-productive laborers go by the name "the intellectuals," "the intelligentsia," or "the highbrows."

None of these names is accurate. It is perhaps better to

say that in a society in which there is unrest and a "sense" of repression, the repressors, the repressed, and the publicists correspond to the exploiters, the exploited, and the intellectuals, respectively.

The small minority of "repressors" can maintain the system of repression only so long as they have the willing support of the publicists. The repressed class, in a society that is ripe for revolution, always outnumbers both of the other classes combined. They can dominate either or both of the other classes whenever they have become sufficiently class conscious and sufficiently organized and disciplined to act collectively. The position of both repressors and publicists is therefore precarious unless the publicists maintain sufficient confidence in the existing régime to give it their loyal support.

No system of repression begins as such. Every system starts as an improvement over the previous system. It commends itself as socially advantageous—otherwise it would not be adopted. But any social system, no matter how excellent at the time of its adoption, is likely to become repressive with the lapse of time and the progress of civilization. A given institution, proving itself to be good, is "sold" to the society by the publicists and becomes an integral part of the social structure. It is sanctioned by law and custom, by religion and ethics. When the institution becomes repressive, the inarticulate masses feel the repression first but do not understand the causes of it. An interval, generally a long one, occurs between the time any institution is first felt to be repressive and the time the publicists lose their faith in it. During such intervals (which cover most of the years of recorded history) the publicists support repressive institutions. But sooner or later the publicists become infected with the prevailing unrest and begin to sympathize with the repressed class. Frequently, after a time the publicists feel the repression themselves. In that case they bestir themselves energetically to discover the cause of the existing unrest. The repressors neither feel the repression nor, except in rare cases, understand its causes. When the publicists are sure that an institution, which they had supposed to be good, is really repressive, they attack that institution with a zeal proportionate to their anger at having been deluded as to its nature. In other words, they desert the cause of the existing institution and support the cause of the institution that is, as they hope and believe, to replace it.

It is to be noted in the discussion of the present-day class conflict that the word "idle" applied to the dominant class means not only inactive but, what is more important, it means the practice of forms of activity conceived to be useless or harmful by a given society at a given time. Similarly, and with the same qualifications, the term "working people" or "working class" embraces not only mechanics and manual laborers, but all persons, except the publicists, engaged in activities considered to be socially useful.

The foregoing discussion perhaps will help to make clear why the "transfer of the allegiance of the publicists" is one of major symptoms of an approaching revolution. A few historical illustrations may aid in bringing out the importance of this "transfer."

The Roman Empire never contained so many great statesmen and able administrators as during the period of its decline and fall. At the very time it was going to pieces, because of defective organization and incompetent government, it produced the most illustrious series of organizers and governors that is known in history. But these men were not in the service of the Empire. They left the Empire to its fate and devoted their genius to the construction of the most perfect institution of social control that the world has ever seen. It is perhaps not extreme to say that if that incomparable succession of statesmen who organized the Catholic church had devoted their abilities with equal zeal to the reorganization of the Roman Empire, that Empire might exist today—and with it a civilization a thousand years in advance of what we have. In any case, the fact that men like Ambrose, Augustine, Jerome, and Leo I transferred their support from the secular government to the church was a sure symptom of the advancing revolution which was to substitute the papacy for the empire.

In the case of the Protestant Reformation the stages in the "transfer" are clear. From John of Paris, D'Ailly, and Gerson through Colet, More, and Erasmus to Luther, Calvin, and Knox the change is evident. First is the desire for administrative reform, then the demand for thoroughgoing reconstruction, and finally the determination to destroy the ancient church altogether. An identical transition of publicists' opinions can be traced in every country that became Protestant.

In the case of the Puritan Revolution in England, even the most careless reader of history cannot help perceiving that the attitude of such publicists as Eliot, Pym, and Hampden foreshadowed the coming of Cromwell and the commonwealth.

In France, in the year 1700, publicists of the most eminent character and ability—men like Bossuet and Fenelon—upheld the doctrine of the divine right of kings. Two generations later there was not a man of intellectual distinction in the kingdom who did not attack that doctrine as false and ridiculous. The importance of the encyclopedists and philosophers as the harbingers of the coming revolution is one of the commonplaces of history.

Adams, Otis, Lee, Franklin, and many other leaders in the American Revolution attained eminence by their support of the cause of liberty at least ten years before the Declaration of Independence. Pitt, Burke, and numerous others in England supported the American publicists. This antagonistic attitude of the publicists portended revolution as early as 1765, if not earlier. If the government of George III had had any reasonable degree of perspicacity it would have recognized the danger signal.

The gradual transfer of the allegiance of the Russian intellectuals can be traced readily for three generations. Gogol and Puskin were more moderate critics of the czardom than Dostoievsky and Tolstoi, who in turn were moderates compared to Kropotkin and Gorki. For decades before its final overthrow, the government of the czars was without a public apologist of even second-rate ability. Had it not been hopelessly blind, it would have perceived in this fact the certainty of its own destruction.[1]

An institution of any size or importance always has enemies. A certain amount of criticism is to be expected, and is no sign of revolution—or of anything else of moment. Then there are the occasional and sporadic outbursts of small groups of intellectuals. These, also, are without importance. But a change of front by the majority of publicists, kept up through a period of years, is a matter of the very first importance. It is both the most easily recognized

[1] See M. Olgin, *The Soul of the Russian Revolution;* also T. G. Masaryk, *The Spirit of Russia*, in which the beginnings of social unrest as manifested by literary and philosophical discussion and ferment among the intellectuals are concretely shown.

symptom of coming upheaval and the most potent cause
of the upheaval which it portends.

When the publicists once decide to support the repressed
class rather than the repressors, there is a decided quicken-
ing in the *tempo* of the revolutionary movement though
everyone is still ignorant that any revolution is to take
place.

One of the first results of the publicists' change of front
is a loss of faith in the individuals who at the time have
control of the society. The intellectuals, though aware of
repression, are not yet aware of its cause. Being angry and
ignorant—to some degree angry because ignorant—they
strike out, childlike, at the most conspicuous persons in
sight. The persons who have control, being the most conspicuous persons, naturally become the objects of the publicists' wrath. All and several are attacked under the impression that all are, or may be, repressors.

The conspicuous individuals under stress of this attack
speedily lose the respect of the public. They are contemned
as dull and uninspiring. Idealism and enthusiasm are no
longer engendered by their purposes or actions. Whatever
they do is esteemed wrong. In more extreme cases these individuals, without regard to personal character and merit,
become objects of popular odium and may be mobbed or
even assassinated.

The publicists and public alike at this stage become
victims of the "good-man" fallacy. They have the idea that
everything will come out all right if only good men are
placed at the head of affairs. Everybody pins his faith on
the good pope, the good king, or the good ruler of some sort.
This fallacy is natural. Institutions that are essentially
sound will work well if good men are placed in control of

them. The whole point about a pre-revolutionary society is that its institutions, or some of them, are essentially unsound, and will not work well no matter who is in control of them. But the publicists do not immediately recognize that this is the condition of their society. They demand the removal of obnoxious, conspicuous persons and their replacement by good men. Sometimes the replacement occurs, sometimes not. The result is the same in either case. The repression, not being due to the faults of individuals, remains in spite of any substitution of good individuals for bad ones. The only result is that the good individuals lose their popularity. Leo X was succeeded by Adrian VI, a good man if there ever was one, but the revolt against the papacy went on just the same. Strafford and Laud were replaced by Falkland and Hyde. The change did no more to save the head of Charles I than the similar substitution of Turgot and Necker for Brienne and Calonne did to save that of Louis XVI.

But in any society in which the majority of the publicists are really in revolt against the existing conditions, the good-man fallacy does not persist very long. It is only a passing phase and generally a short one.

The publicists presently discover that the real cause of the unrest is to be found in certain archaic elements of the social order. The archaism generally, perhaps always, is embodied in some group or order of men, who are forthwith brought into prominence and then into condemnation as representatives of the archaic institutions. The publicists, having ascertained the identity of the delinquent institutions, start what is essentially an "advertising offensive" against them. The technique is in general the same as that of a political campaign. Often it begins as a political campaign, though it does not end as one. A political campaign is in some respects a sort of small-bore, blank-cartridge imitation of a revolution. The people in a political campaign do not really care how it comes out. Both sides agree beforehand to abide the issue no matter which side wins, because the issue is essentially unimportant and does not involve their elemental wishes. A revolution is like a political campaign in which no such previous agreement is made. People really do care how it comes out because their elemental wishes are involved. A revolution therefore contains an important psychological ingredient lacking in a political campaign, but within fairly wide limits the operative technique at this stage is the same.

An essential step in the development of revolution is the gradual concentration of public dissatisfaction upon some one institution and the persons representing it. Before any institution can become either very popular or very unpopular public attention must be fixed on it—and must stay fixed. In the earlier stages of a revolutionary movement the dissatisfaction is diffused and dissipated. All sorts of institutions—the political government, the educational system, the church, the economic organization, and many others—are growled about and criticized. Because the discontent is directed against too many and too diverse objects, it is rendered both feeble and futile. One great service which the publicists render to the revolutionary movement is that of concentrating the general irritation which is spending itself thus wastefully. They focus the discontent against some one institution or class and keep it focused there. The institution or class in question becomes the object of popular antagonism to the exclusion of all other institutions or classes.

The real test of the intellect of the intellectuals comes at just this point. They may make a mistake. They may concentrate public anger on the wrong institution or class—on a class or institution not really the cause of the repression. In such a case revolutionary effort runs up a blind alley, reaction follows this futility, and the whole movement must be redirected at great cost of time and effort.

At this point, similarly, there occurs one of the best opportunities of the repressors to avert, or at least postpone, revolution. If they can succeed in diverting the attention of the repressed classes to some other group or institution which is not to blame for the repression, and if they can arouse sufficient animosity against this other institution so that an attack is made upon it, they can save their class and the institution they represent for a long time—at least two or three generations. In cases where there are still able publicists in the service of the threatened institution, and in cases where the intellectuals are still uncertain as to what is the cause of repression, these tactics are likely to prove successful.

This study is concerned primarily with those great revolutions which have succeeded. Still one instance of a cleverly diverted and postponed revolution may not come amiss.

In England, as in other countries, in the early part of the fifteenth century, widespread discontent was generated by the evils of the church. Three Parliaments within fifteen years urged the king to seize all the property of the church and apply it to the costs of the civil government. They insisted that the church possessed a third of all the lands of the kingdom, that it contributed nothing to the public expenses, and that this great wealth disqualified the clergy from performing their ministerial functions with proper zeal and attention. There was much truth in these contentions. The people of England did suffer from the serious abuses then existing in the church. But the clergy were not lacking in shrewdness and intelligence. They aroused the ambitions of the warlike king, Henry V, to conquer France. They represented to Parliament the enormous booty and great prestige to be gained for England by such a conquest. They aroused the war spirit of the common people by sermons and exhortations. Their efforts succeeded. The war against France was undertaken. That war was successful; almost the whole of France was conquered. The enormous booty gained and the splendor of the great victory at Agincourt entirely monopolized popular attention. The revolutionary movement against the church was postponed for more than a century.

King James I had a similar opportunity to divert the Puritan Revolution when Parliament urged him to raise a powerful army and intervene in support of the Protestants in the Thirty Years' War. Had he done so—and had he been victorious—as might well have happened, the Stuart dream of an absolute monarchy would very likely have been achieved. The Puritan Revolution might have been nearly contemporary with that of France.

To divert popular attention from domestic repressions by starting a foreign war is one of the oldest tricks of statecraft. There is some reason to believe that the Russian czardom may have had this ancient trick in mind when it entered the late war. But they may have forgotten that for the trick to succeed it is essential that the war be successful. Defeat in foreign war hastens revolution, as it did in this case.

Orgiastic excitement—dances, festivals, and religious movements—are sometimes substitutes for foreign war, as the outlet for popular discontent. Emotional energy and mental energy have this in common. There is only so much of them. If they are exhausted in one way they are not available in another—at least not until there has been time for recuperation. If the late czardom, instead of abolishing vodka, had made it very plentiful and very cheap—if, in addition, they had stimulated to the utmost those forms of religious frenzy and excitement to which the Russian populace appear to be so susceptible—then it is at least possible that the people would have been so exhausted mentally, emotionally, and financially by their alcoholic and religious orgies that they would not have had sufficient energy left to carry out a successful revolution.

All of this may seem very theoretical, as indeed it is. But with the development of the technique of government propaganda, some such orgiastic substitution for revolution may well come within the range of the practical politics of the not distant future. In the United States, Volsteadism and Fundamentalism exhaust mental and moral energies which might otherwise be directed against certain serious governmental scandals.

The manner in which the publicists focus the public attention on the repressive class is worth noticing; by and large, the method is that of popularizing scandal. If the newspapers of the world are any evidence, the public seems to have an insatiable appetite for scandal. It is easiest to concentrate public interest on that class in society that is most conspicuous. The repressors are that class. Social unrest makes news for the same reason that it makes politics. It is out of the general discontent that political issues arise.

The publicists have a "flair for news." A flair for news includes the ability to discover scandal. The dominant class is inevitably a shining mark if for no other reason than merely because it is conspicuous. A due regard for the increase of their own influence, prestige, power, and emolument naturally leads the intelligentsia to concentrate their efforts upon the "exposure" of that class.

The repressive class is thereupon subjected to the most pitiless investigation and publicity. It becomes the object of the most pervading and merciless gossip. Its weakness and its failures, its ignorance and stupidities, its sins and its shames, its vices and its crimes, its heartlessness and its frivolity, are dwelt upon—not once or twice but a hundred and a thousand times. No class of people is ever subjected to such complete exposure and such terrific attack as the dominant class in a pre-revolutionary society. There is naturally in such exposures a large element of truth uncovered. But every scandal substantiated by facts is enlarged and exaggerated through constant repetition. Every publicist seeks to outdo his colleagues in the quantity and quality of his "muck-raking." The more startling and exciting the conditions exposed, the more eagerly it is seized upon by the public and the greater is the author's prestige. This is true not only of the publicists as a class but of all the individuals who retail the scandals throughout the society. It comes about, therefore, that in addition to the scandals that are true, and to those that are exaggerated, others are added which have no basis in fact at all. Rumors of the wildest kind are readily circulated and as readily believed. There is nothing unnatural or unusual about this. The growth of scandal and rumor is a most ordinary phenomenon observable in all societies at all times. Under ordinary circumstances it is a matter of small importance. The persons and institutions attacked are so numerous and so heterogeneous, the succession of them is so rapid, that the result is negligible. In a pre-revolutionary society the importance of scandal and rumor arises from the fact that the same class is subjected to them over a long period. As a result of sheer repetition, exaggerated scandals and baseless rumors come to be believed as facts, and these have an influence on public opinion much greater than that of the simple truth.

The attacks on the dominant classes by the publicists often attain a high level of literary and forensic excellence— as might be expected when able and eloquent men are deeply stirred by manifest wrongs. This "literature of exposure" is one of the most characteristic symptoms of a coming revolution, and naturally it continues in ever increasing volume during the course of the revolution until the position of the obnoxious class and the institutions they represent is completely undermined.

It is not necessary to do more than mention one or two examples of these attacks. In the Puritan Revolution, the Marprelate tracts and the Grand Remonstrance are two illustrations among thousands. The American Declaration of Independence is a summary of numerous "declarations" and "resolutions" put out in all the colonies from the time of the famous "Five Resolutions" of Patrick Henry in 1765 onward. The collection of speeches, pamphlets, sermons, articles, poems, dialogues, plays, and literature of all sorts attacking the royal government that were published before the outbreak of the Revolution makes a considerable library. For some reason the attacks made upon religious repressors are especially numerous and voluminous. The attacks of the publicists upon the church and the priesthood go back for centuries before the Reformation, and are of a most appalling bulk. They comprise tens of thousands, if not hundreds of thousands, of separate publications. The attacks of the early Christians upon the pagan religion and pagan society have, in great part, perished in the course of the centuries. Enough remains, however, to fill a goodly number of stout volumes.

When the publicists launch this attack upon the repressive class an enormous amount of discussion ensues. Many of the so-called "repressors" are personally men of kindly and benevolent character. They have their relatives, friends, and dependents who rally to their defense. Much of the scandal published, being either false or exaggerated, is refuted by those attacked and those in a position to know the facts. But there is not at this time any sharp division into two parties or factions. Instead, there are a great number of ill-defined, inchoate groups not very certain as to the extent of their own agreement. Everybody considers that reform is desirable, or at least necessary. As to the kind and degree of reform there are numerous gradations of opinion—as there are also over the question of how the reform can be best accomplished. It is to be noted that the only idea is reform. There is no purpose, or even thought, of revolution. That idea is entirely absent, or very remote, from the minds of the persons engaged in discussion. It never even comes up for discussion, except, possibly, when suggested by a very few extreme radicals who are too far in advance of public sentiment to be of importance. As the discussion continues and so many different points of view are disclosed, the persons holding the most divergent opinions sometimes go beyond the stage of verbal conflict. Social and economic antagonisms begin to show themselves.

Friendships are broken. Business boycotts are instituted. Even family disunion appears. The repressive classes and their supporters are subject to various kinds of social pressure—even ostracism.

The deluge of pamphlets, poems, plays, and literary productions of all sorts is only the most visible part of the attack on the repressive class. It is by no means all of it, nor perhaps the most important part of it. Discussion takes place also among the great "unprinting masses"—the people who form their opinions from conversation instead of from reading. These people are commonly forgotten, but their influence, especially in the crises of revolution, is important. The attack of the publicists causes the repressors to defend themselves as best they can. They reply both by writing and by word of mouth. It is soon evident that their defense is feeble. Even when, as at first, they and their supporters may be in a numerical majority, they are weak because they are held together only by a traditional, unthinking loyalty to existing institutions. In the course of the discussion on reform this loyalty suffers great attrition until in great numbers of men only a shell of custom remains—though they frequently are unaware of the fact.

It is needless to give any extensive examples of the reformist discussions which go on for months and years in every pre-revolutionary society after the publicists concentrate popular attention on the evils of that society. Origen and Celsus debate Christianity and paganism—a type of thousands and tens of thousands of lesser debates going on in ancient Roman society. Luther and Eck hold a great disputation about the Catholic church—the sign and symbol of the innumerable religious discussions which characterized the whole of Western civilization at the time. So many thou-

sands of argumentative pamphlets were issued during the
period preceding the Puritan Revolution that, in the words
of Green, they "turned England at large into a school of
political discussion."[1]   The arguments and debates about
colonial liberty, both in England and America, for years before the American Revolution are chronicled in every school-
book of American history. If Johnson's *Taxation No Tyranny* is not so well known as Burke's *Plea for Conciliation*, it
only proves that even the greatest arguer could do little for
such a bad cause. Even under the extreme repression of the
czardom a notable period of discussion followed the attacks
of the great publicists on the autocracy. The Duma, established after the abortive uprising of 1905, was chiefly useful
as a discussion club. But the discussions of reform in the
Duma were by no means isolated phenomena. Similar discussions both in print and verbally went on during a dozen
years all over Russia, and indeed all over the civilized world.
Reformist discussion is, in short, a symptom discoverable
in every pre-revolutionary society.

During this long period of discussion an important
psychological change takes place in the repressed classes.
This change is an enormous development of what Miller
calls the "oppression psychosis," which is the obsession that
there is nothing much in the world except oppression; that
the only object of life is to fight oppression. It is an attitude
of mind that is always looking for trouble. Groups dominated by it always "have a chip on the shoulder." They are
always expecting slights, disparagements, and injustices.
They see oppression even where there is none. They become
violently self-assertive at the least opportunity. The oppression psychosis is important in the revolutionary process be-

[1] *History of the English People*, Book VII, chap. viii.

cause it turns the previous more or less passive discontent of the repressed group into the active emotion of hate of the repressors. Hatred of a common enemy is the most powerful known agency for producing group unity. The publicists, by their previous attack, have pointed out the repressors as the common enemy. The discontent of the repressed at their lot turns into hatred of the repressors, because the discussion of reform, which goes on for a long time, gets nowhere. It is, in the nature of the case, impossible that it should get anywhere. The case is one in which a large group of socially useful people are deprived of due honor, wealth, dignity, prestige, social rank, political power, ease, comfort, luxury, and all the other good things of this life, while a small group of socially useless people possess a superabundance of all these good things. The only solution is to deprive the socially useless people of all their good things and bestow them upon the socially useful people. This cannot be done by discussion, voting, or any other sort of parliamentary procedure. Neither party will abide the issue of the parliamentary process. If those who possess all the good things are outdiscussed or outvoted, they will fight to keep their possessions. If those who are deprived of the good things are outdiscussed or outvoted, they will fight to get possession of them. The long pre-revolutionary discussion is thus predestined to failure.

But the failure of the discussion is the failure of the repressed class. This failure generates in their minds the oppression psychosis. They have the better of the discussion, but no matter how completely they triumph in argument, the repressors continue in possession of the good things. During the discussion the repressed class prove the fact that they are suffering injustice. But they obtain no redress. Obtaining no redress they naturally come to hate those who profit by the injustice from which they suffer. They consider the repressors to be the authors of the injustice—though the injustice, as a matter of fact, is due to archaic social arrangements.

All repressed groups in pre-revolutionary societies develop this oppression psychosis, its concomitant hatred of the repressors, and group solidarity. The writings of the early Christians against the pagans show this very plainly. The intemperate violence of much of their controversial literature against the evils of ancient civilization is notorious, and has deservedly subjected them to the accusation of neglecting that brotherly love which it was their first duty as Christians to practice. In one of these controversial writings, the *De spectaculis* of Tertullian, occurs the famous statement that the principal joy of the Christians in the hereafter will be to stand upon the ramparts of heaven and gaze down upon the tortures of the pagans writhing in the flames of hell. In defense of Christianity be it said that the provocation for this statement justified it if any provocation ever could. Two young Christian girls, one of them a relative of Tertullian, had been stripped naked in the arena of a crowded amphitheater, publicly violated in the sight of thousands of spectators, and then torn to pieces by wild beasts. Perhaps even a Father of the Church like Tertullian may be pardoned for wishing evil to the perpetrators of such a deed.

The growth of the oppression psychosis in the opponents of the papacy during the pre-reformation period is familiar to all students of church history. Illustrations are to be found in *The Ship of Fools*, in *The Letters of Obscure Men*, and in many of the writings of Erasmus. In the period preceding the Puritan Revolution the famous *Histriomastix* is only an outstanding example of the psychology of the whole Puritan group. The authorization of innocent and healthy outdoor games after church on Sunday was considered to be a wicked plot to destroy all true religion. The touchiness and irritability of Voltaire and so many other French philosophers is at least in part due to the oppression psychosis. The numerous hindrances and delays to which the various Parliaments subjected the edicts of Louis XVI can be largely ascribed to the same cause. The fantastic legends of the Parc-aux-Cerfs and the baths of children's blood show, at a still earlier time, the grotesque and horrible development of this psychosis among the masses of the people.

In the thirteen American colonies before the Revolution, the psychosis is well illustrated in Dickinson's *Letters of a Farmer*. The enormous popularity of these *Letters* proves how accurately they reflected the mood of the people. The growing irritation and sensitiveness of the colonial assemblies to any exercise of the royal prerogative without their approval is another instance of the same disposition. Dr. Johnson, in his *Taxation No Tyranny*, proposed that the negro slaves be freed and provided with agricultural implements to enable them to earn their living as farmers. The proposal, in itself, was humane and possibly intelligent.[1] It was construed to be an advocacy of a negro rebellion and the massacre of the plantation owners by their slaves.

Another technique employed by the publicists in the course of the pre-revolutionary discussion greatly aids the growth of the oppression psychosis. This technique consists in putting a very great stress upon the worth and value of

[1] Lossing, *The Pictorial Field Book of the Revolution*, II, 375.

the repressed class. Their importance is brought out in the clearest light. History is ransacked to provide them with an illustrious background. Their cause is linked up with the famous popular revolutions of all ages. The events of past time are interpreted as a preparation for their advent to power. Their virtues are exaggerated. Their faults are minimized or entirely overlooked. They are provided with a common body of tradition and a long list of heroes, largely manufactured *ad hoc*. However apocryphal this common body of tradition may be, it serves to give the repressed class a feeling of dignity and self-respect. It is an important factor in promoting their unity, and of reinforcing the solidarity produced by the more powerful emotion of hatred of the repressors. The more their sense of their own importance increases the greater appears the wickedness of their repression and the more keenly they resent any sign of that repression.

The early Christians were thus morally reinforced by the great body of Old Testament tradition and considered themselves the "chosen people," even as the Jews in an earlier age. Those who opposed the papacy in pre-reformation days justified themselves as the restorers of the pure doctrine and practice of the early Christians. The Puritans, like the early Christians, fortified themselves with the Old Testament tradition and considered themselves similarly as the "chosen people" of God. The French in their pre-revolutionary period had recourse to the classical revolutionary tradition as was fitting in a Latin people. They considered Cato, Brutus, the Gracchi, and other ancient worthies to be at once their prototypes and their models. The American pre-revolutionary publicists employed both the classical and the English traditions. In the famous words of Patrick

Henry: "Caesar had his Brutus, Charles I, his Cromwell and George III—may profit by their example."

During this discussion period the repressors gradually lose faith in themselves and in their cause. They continue to hold possession of all the good things of life, but they come to question the justice of their title to them. The case for the repressed class is a strong one. It is ably presented by the publicists. It is argued at great length and in minute detail, and it produces its effect despite the continuance of the repressors in power. Those of the repressors who are intelligent and open minded admit that the existing conditions are unjust and intolerable. They do not wish them to continue, even though they may be opposed to violent or sudden change. Others, though they still defend the system of repression, do so half-heartedly and with no great enthusiasm or self-confidence. A certain number of repressors, the most narrow-minded and least-intelligent ones, react the other way. They become more convinced than ever of the indefeasible righteousness of the repressive régime. These defenders of abuses are mentally incapable of a rational defense of their opinions. But this bothers them not at all, since they commonly rest their case on some super-rational ground such as the "divine right" of kings or the "sacredness" of property. They become reactionary, and get so out of touch with contemporary ideas that they lose all influence except with the most ignorant and superstitious sections of the population, such as the peasantry of remote districts.

So long as the entire body of repressors believe firmly in themselves and in the righteousness of their actions, they cannot be overthrown by revolution. They possess all the power of government and law, all the prestige of authority and position, and all the sanction of religion and morals. These advantages are sufficient to enable them to retain their position for some time even after their morale has become low. When their morale is high these same advantages are decisive in making their position secure. Being confident of their own right, they possess all the agencies for begetting a like confidence in the rest of society. Under such conditions their rule is firm. They make decisions promptly and carry them out vigorously. They are courageous, both in war and in the conduct of civil government. The army respects and obeys them because they exhibit both military ability and personal bravery. They are the most capable people in the society, and bear rule because of that fact. Their rule is to a serious degree repressive of the legitimate elemental wishes of the lower classes, yet it seems certain that, on the whole, their social usefulness is still sufficient to justify their retention of power. All ruling classes pass through this period when they are both repressive and self-confident. Such a period is generally seen at its best about halfway between the beginning and the end of the domination of the class concerned.

Christianity was by no means the first Eastern religion which attempted to dislodge Roman paganism in Western Europe. Early in the second century B.C. Bacchus worship was introduced from Asia Minor. It made great headway in Rome, and rapidly spread throughout Italy as well as to other parts of the republic. But the rulers of the Rome of that age believed sincerely in their native gods and in the necessity of maintaining the ancient national worship. A decree of the Senate was issued against the new foreign religion. Its assemblies were broken up. Its places of worship were destroyed. Thousands of its adherents were put to death. Other thousands were forced to recant and were banished. Within a short time it was extirpated.

The Albigenses certainly had as good cause to revolt against the papacy as had the Protestants of a later time. But the Catholic church of the thirteenth century believed in itself. It was firm in its theological doctrines, and its clergy were proudly conscious of their great function as the upholders of justice and the maintainers of social order. The pope, Innocent III, was the most able ruler then alive. He was firm, intelligent, and shrewd. He had plenty of confidence both in himself and in his cause, and he was able to inspire like confidence in others. The result was that he had no great difficulty in putting down the revolt. The crusade against the Albigenses was exceedingly cruel and bloody, but it was short, and it ended in the total destruction of the heretical movement.

The Jacquerie, the French peasant revolt of 1358, was a formidable uprising. It was associated with and aided by a revolt in the city of Paris. The peasants were numerous and infuriated by oppression. Yet the whole revolt, so far as the peasants were concerned, was put down in a very short time, scarcely more than a month. King Charles the Bad of Navarre, who commanded the forces of the nobility, was a courageous man, an able general, and a skilful diplomat—in spite of all his faults. The Count Gaston de Foix and the Captal de Buch, the two other leaders of the aristocracy, were renowned knights whose fame is still preserved in song and story. The order of chivalry which produced such men was indeed in full bloom, but not yet in decay. The French nobility of the fourteenth century believed in themselves and in feudalism. In spite of the way they oppressed the serfs, they were the ablest men in the society of the time. They put down the revolt speedily, bloodily, and effectually.

The government of Queen Elizabeth of England was highly autocratic and repressive. It put down all opposition, whether of Puritans or Roman Catholics, with an iron hand. But it was an able government, far sighted, shrewd, and brave. It was a government which numbered among its members the most competent persons in the country—beginning with the Queen herself. It was performing an essential public service in saving England from foreign invasion and from civil war. It was very conscious of its own value and very certain of its usefulness to society. It was able to put down without trouble, almost without striking a blow, three insurrections supported by large sections of the people, animated by religious zeal.

Bacon's Rebellion in Virginia in 1667 was as much justified by tryanny and misgovernment as was the American Revolution of one hundred years later. Bacon was a popular and skilful leader. Great numbers of the colonists sympathized with his cause, which was identically the same as that of 1776. He was for a time successful. Yet Governor Berkeley, in spite of his personal unpopularity and that of his government, was able very quickly to stamp out the rebellion with the aid of troops from England.

The fact is that until 1763 the royal governors maintained their authority, arbitrary as it often was, with relatively little trouble. When necessary they sent for British troops to maintain their authority, and this met with only very slight complaint from the colonists. The reason, of course, was that until 1763 royal governors and British troops were useful and even necessary people. The colonists were in constant danger of attack from the Indians and from the French. Royal governors with real power and able to summon the aid of British troops in time of danger were essential to the peace and welfare, if not to the very existence of the colonies. The governors and their soldiers knew this, and to their credit be it said they did their job well, if roughly. The Indians were driven back, the French colonies in Canada were conquered, and all danger of external attack removed. Until the time this task was accomplished the royal governors with the aid of British soldiers were able to put down revolt with great ease.

Since no revolution against a ruling class can be successful so long as they have confidence in themselves and faith in what they stand for, it is important to note the method employed by the publicists in destroying their faith and self-confidence. The fact is that the repressors, no less than the repressed, depend upon the intellectuals for their ideas. The intellectuals are the professional custodians of education, morality, and religion. It is their job to make and unmake right and wrong, good and bad, vice and virtue, morality and immorality, nobleness and depravity, orthodoxy and heresy, sense and foolishness. They are limited in this great task by the state of economic development in the society concerned, and by the extent of the social unrest that for any reason exists at the time. But within this limit they can do very much as they please, provided they are willing to work hard enough and long enough.

No sooner do the publicists espouse the cause of the repressed class than they proceed to put forth, and to popularize by discussion, a new body of knowledge and a new code of morals, including new standards of wisdom and foolishness. This new teaching is designed, among other things, to make the repressors ridiculous in their own eyes as well as in the eyes of everyone else. Unless it succeeds in doing this, the revolution is likely to be postponed. If it is not postponed, it will be abortive. A ruling class can survive even though it knows itself to be tyrannical. It cannot survive if it is made to appear foolish in its own sight. Repressors, in order to retain power, will continue to do conscious evil for a long time. They will not long continue to do things they know to be silly. The most effective argument against any form of repression is not that it is wicked or even sinful, but that it is foolish and ridiculous. This argument will "get under the skin" of the repressors when all others fail. The condition of repression which exists in any society before a great revolution really is stupid and silly when looked at rationally, just as it is tyrannical and unjust when regarded emotionally. Nothing undermines authority so completely as making it ridiculous—particularly to itself. Since both the repressors and their system of repression actually are ridiculous it is a relatively easy matter to show them to be so, and the intellectuals have a fine time doing it.

Origen, Augustine, and the rest of the early Church Fathers are dull and heavy reading for the most part, but not entirely. They are interesting and humorous, even today, when they ridicule the puerilities and absurdities of the classical mythology. In the later days of Roman paganism its priests winked at one another while performing its sacrifices. They no longer believed that the condition of a chicken's liver should determine the conduct of public affairs. It was not long before they abandoned a religion which indulged in such absurdities.

The Ship of Fools, The Letters of Obscure Men, and similar satires did more to undermine respect for the medieval church than all the solemn tomes setting forth its iniquities.

It is not a mere coincidence that the Reformation began in the pontificate of Leo X, who declared that Christianity was a profitable superstition for ecclesiastics. The very words "hocus-pocus" (for *Hoc est Corpus*—the most sacred words in the mass) show how ridicule succeeded in undermining a whole religious system. The word "dunce" is another proof of the same thing. It is derived from Duns Scotus; Duns was a theologian of the highest repute in the medieval church.

Even a casual examination of the enormous pamphlet literature which preceded the Puritan Revolution will convince anyone that the Puritans, in spite of their reputation for extreme solemnity, were by no means lacking in wit, shrewdness, and the power of making their opponents ridiculous. They seem to have recognized and exposed the absurdity of every form of superstition except their own. In the light of their robust common sense the doctrine of the divine right of kings came to appear incredible and fantastic. The Cavaliers, brave and gallant as they were, bear to this day the brand put upon them by the Puritans—the brand of being roistering and foppish spendthrifts, unfit for the administration of important business. The current American concept of aristocracy comes by direct descent from the Puritans. According to this concept, aristocracy, in addition to being intrinsically inequitable, is intrinsically irrational and ludicrous. By this simple process of making the then-ruling class appear foolish and frivolous, the Puritans, did more to weaken the Stuart despotism than by all their solemn declarations about royal tyranny.

The American colonies might, perhaps, have tolerated the government of an autocrat who was a capable ruler. They could not tolerate the government of an autocrat who was a blockhead. The great point made by the publicists,

both in England and America, was that the British government, in its dealings with the colonies, was perverse and
foolish. The verdict of these famous publicists has been upheld by history. That verdict is that George III was not
so much cruel as stupid. He was more a dunce than a ty-
rant. A long series of actions, at once provocative and
puerile, destroyed all respect for regal authority. The
Americans finally overthrew it, as much because of its hopeless lack of intelligence as because of its actual misdeeds.
Even if the American Revolution had not put an end to
George III's silly attempt at autocratic government, the
English people themselves would presently have done so.
But it was the public's belief in its folly rather than in its
wickedness which destroyed it.

In the pre-revolutionary societies of France and Russia
the process of undermining the self-confidence of the ruling
classes was so similar that both countries can be considered
together. In both we see a feeble autocrat, a decadent nobility, and an un-Christlike church exploiting a great and
powerful people. The situation was such, in each case, as to
offer unlimited scope for satire and ridicule. In each case a
whole succession of clever and able publicists took full advantage of the extraordinary opportunity. In both countries the effect was the same. The more enlightened and
capable members of the ruling class openly scoffed at the
absurdity of the institutions to which they owed their own
eminence. The conviction of the essential silliness of the
ancient system of repression prevented its intelligent beneficiaries in either nation from making any real effort to
prevent its overthrow. The unintelligent beneficiaries could
do nothing. Louis XV uttered the prophetic words: "Après
moi, le déluge." Nicholas II was too stupid to say anything.

SELECTED REFERENCES

GREEN, JOHN RICHARD. *History of the English People*, Book VII, chap. viii. New York, 1881.

LOSSING, BENSON J. *The Pictorial Field-Book of the Revolution*, Vol. II, New York, 1860.

LEWIS, WYNDHAM. *The Art of Being Ruled*, chap. v. New York, 1926.

LIPPMANN, WALTER. *The Phantom Public*. New York, 1925.

LORIA, ACHILLE. *Economic Foundations of Society*, chap. iv. Translated from the 2d French ed. by LINDLEY M. KEASBEY. New York, 1899.

MASARYK, TOMÁŠ G. *The Spirit of Russia, Studies in History, Literature and Philosophy*. New York, 1919.

MILLER, HERBERT A. *Races, Nations and Classes*, "The Psychology of Domination and Freedom," chap. iv. Philadelphia and London, 1924.

MOMMSEN, THEODOR. *History of Rome*, Vol. III, chap. xiii. New York, 1869–70.

MUNRO, DANA CARLETON. *The Middle Ages*, chaps. ii and iv. New York, 1921.

OLGIN, MOISSAYE J. *The Soul of the Russian Revolution*. New York, 1917.

PARISET, G. *La Révolution*, Vol. II, in ERNEST LAVISSE, *Histoire de France contemporaine depuis la révolution Jusqu'à la paix de 1919*. Paris, 1920–22.

VICKERS, KENNETH H. *England in the Later Middle Ages* (3d ed.). chap. xviii. London, 1921.

CHAPTER V

THE ECONOMIC INCENTIVE AND THE SOCIAL MYTH

If social phenomena are to be considered at all, it is necessary to consider them in some order. So in the preceding chapter a number of the more serious symptoms of revolution were dealt with seriatim. But they do not occur seriatim. Many of them occur, or seem to occur, simultaneously, or nearly so. Each of them is a process as well as a symptom, and each of them has a more or less definite duration. In addition, each of them influences and is influenced by all of the others, and all of them are controlled in some measure by a large number of outside forces not now under consideration.

The preceding sketch is therefore much more simple and diagrammatic than the reality it attempts to analyze. The sequence of symptoms might be given differently and other symptoms included without affecting the point of the argument. All that is contended is that these symptoms do show themselves and can be observed by any competent person on the lookout for them. An endeavor has been made to present them somewhat in the order in which they begin to assume importance in the history, but that is all. Most of them may be observed, at least in initial form, for some time before they become obviously evident. They continue to manifest themselves, in most cases, up to the outbreak of the revolution and beyond. Any given symptom may become prominent, then recede, then become prominent again, and continue to repeat this process. The symptoms are of very different degrees of importance, both as symptoms and as causes. No technique exists at present for measuring, with any approximation to accuracy, their absolute or even their relative importance. The apparatus for measuring social movements is in a very primitive state of development. Even if it were in a far more advanced state than it is, persons skilful enough from knowledge and long experience to use it successfully would still be lacking. All that can be done at present is to assume that a revolutionary process exists and that it is susceptible of measurement when—if ever —social science possesses tools of sufficient accuracy to do the work. Even this is a hypothesis. But it is a hypothesis which it is necessary to make unless revolution is to be thought of as a phenomenon outside of the natural order. Unless revolution is supernatural, it must be assumed to be explicable, measurable, and predictable—at least in theory.

The preceding chapter dealt with a number of pre-revolutionary symptoms which are coincident with and dependent upon the transfer of the allegiance of the intellectual class from the repressors to the repressed. Two more such symptoms remain to be considered which are of sufficient importance to warrant a somewhat more extended treatment. One of these, the emergence of the economic incentive, would, in all probability, manifest itself even if, conceivably, no intellectual class existed—though, in fact, no human society entirely devoid of an intellectual class has ever been discovered. The other symptom, the social myth, is the pure product of intellectualist activity.

Without adopting too rigidly the doctrine of economic determinism, it may be stated with a considerable degree of assurance that no great historical revolution has ever succeeded without the assistance of the economic incentive.

Human cupidity must be appealed to in order to arouse the energy, the aggressiveness, and the sustained interest of masses of people—without which no revolution can succeed. This is true of the most idealistic, religious revolutions no less than of the most frankly economic ones. Revolution involves the disintegration of society. The evils of this disintegration are so many and so obvious that men are willing to incur them only under stress of the strongest incentives. Whatever may be thought about the power of different incentives, it must be admitted that the economic incentive is not the weakest one.

Although the economic incentive may not assume formal and recognized importance until a relatively late period of pre-revolutionary development, it seems probable that it is the earliest in point of origin of all the revolutionary incentives. In its first form it is negative—mere discontent on the part of the repressed class at their own economic condition. In every society there is discontent at poverty and envy of the rich by the poor. At the earliest stage at which any revolutionary symptoms are observable it does not appear that the envy of the repressed class for their oppressors is in any degree unusual. But it soon becomes very evident and continually increases, reaching its highest point early in the revolutionary outbreak. Before that time it is changed into, or perhaps reinforced by, hatred of the repressors. With this hatred comes the determination to confiscate the wealth of the repressors at the first opportunity. Even fairly reliable statistics on this matter are unavailable except in France and Russia. But it is at least a curious coincidence that in those two countries the peasants owned almost exactly one-third of the agricultural land at the outbreak of the revolutions. In both cases they had been adding largely to their holdings during the generation or two preceding the revolutions. In both cases, also, their eagerness to own the land increased by what it fed on. The greater the amount of land they got into their possession, the stronger was their desire for more. In both cases this "hunger for land" which animated the peasantry seems to have been the ultimate power which determined the success of the revolutions and defeated the forces of reaction.

The peasants, being activated only by the economic motive, do not bother themselves with any aspects of revolution except those connected with their fight to get the land. As soon as they get it, they are willing to allow any form of control to step in which does not imperil their new property rights. But any form of reaction which seems, even in the remotest degree, to threaten their acquisitions is absolutely prohibited.

It should not be inferred that the economic incentive to revolution is merely base and selfish. At its worst it is a desire for a better economic order. It is at the same time, and perhaps mainly so, a desire for status. The repressed class who desire more property seek it not merely as a material value, but because it is a symbol which confers prestige. The property they wish to seize is in the hands of owners, some of them mere parasites, whose ownership of property is detrimental to the welfare of everybody but themselves. Indeed, in a larger social sense, it may be, and often is, argued that the confiscation of the property of the repressors is not only beneficial to the society as a whole, but is beneficial to the repressors themselves, who, so far as they survive, are forced to become productive laborers—a change of condition which may fairly be interpreted as an ethical advance even if it involves a lowering of their social status. An idle and luxurious countess, forced by a revolution to take up stenography or dressmaking for a living, does not occupy so prominent a social position as formerly, but there is no doubt about the fact that she is a more useful member of society. She earns her keep—which is more than she ever did before.

Even though the confiscation of the property of the parasitic repressors may be and is regarded by the revolutionists as essentially just and moral, it can be made to seem so only by a revision of the ethical code prevailing in the older order of society.

This revision of the morals of ownership is one of the most interesting of the pre-revolutionary processes. This justification is invariably a reassertion and application of the principle that the only ultimately valid title to ownership is that the owner can do more for the general welfare by his ownership than can anyone else. On this principle, if any change of ownership, by confiscation or otherwise, promotes the general welfare, it is morally and socially justifiable and will ultimately prevail. That it will prevail in spite of all legal, ethical, and religious codes teaching the contrary, and in spite of any amount of physical force used to back up such codes, is an article of revolutionary faith. The greater the physical force used to back up any system of property not based on the social utility principle, the greater the ferocity of the revolution, if it occurs, by which that system of property is destroyed.

A very simple case of the pre-revolutionary revision of the morals of property will illustrate the process. A Russian peasant by hard work and extreme thrift has been able to purchase one-third enough land to enable him to live decently according to his standard. He desires to own three times as much land as he has. The man from whom he has to get it

is a grand duke who rents the land to the peasant and perhaps squanders the rent upon an actress of dubious morals
in Moscow or Paris. The peasant finds the price of land to be
such that even by the hardest labor and most extreme econ-
omy he can never obtain the land he so eagerly desires and
which he needs to maintain a decent standard of living.
Dull as he is, this fact sets him to thinking, and presently
there dawns on his mind the question of the justification of
ownership. Why should the grand duke own so many thousands of acres while he, the peasant, owns less than a score?
The grand duke does no work on the land. He rarely even
visits his large property. More than likely he never does any
work of any kind. Yet he lives in luxury because he owns
the land. He, the peasant, works hard every day, but is poor
because he does not own the land. His priest teaches him
that it is the "will of God" that the grand duke should own
the land. It is also obvious to the peasant that soldiers will
come and kill him if he tries to take any of the grand duke's
land without paying whatever price the grand duke asks. In
spite of all this, the peasant gradually works out in his mind
the idea that the land should belong to him because he works
on it and makes it productive. After a while he goes a step
farther in his reasoning. If the land should belong to him and
his fellow-peasants, then the grand duke is a robber for keep-
ing the land. This idea that the grand duke is a robber,
holding land that rightly belongs to the peasants, becomes
firmly fixed after a time and colors all the peasant's thinking.
He has never so much as heard the name of the French philosopher, Proudhon, yet in his own particular case of the
grand duke and the land he has arrived at the same conclusion as that famous man: "La propriété c'est le vol." If his
village priest were more informed, he could tell the peasant

that this same idea that "property is robbery" was held by Christianity in its great early days, and that the peasant had rediscovered the teaching of the most holy saints and doctors of the church—St. Jerome, for example, or St. Chrysostom, whose icons are in all the churches. The peasant hears nothing of all this. But presently he does hear, from his cousin who works in a factory in Moscow, that the great Prince Peter Kropotkin in the Czar's very palace had said that peasants should have the land and have it without payment. The Czar put him in prison but he has escaped out of Russia, and there are many other great ones who want the peasant to have the land. This fires the peasant's imagination. He begins to dream of a day when somehow, with the aid of people in the great city who think as he does, he will be able to get his land from that big robber the grand duke and no soldiers will come to kill him for it. If only there is a chance that the soldiers will not come he will run the risk and take the land.

This, or something very like this, was the actual mental process that went on in the heads of millions of illiterate Russian peasants in the generations preceding the Revolution. Without knowing anything about socialism, syndicalism, anarchism, or any other radical theory whatever, the peasant was prepared by 1917 to act with any revolutionary group in the cities, if only they would help him get the land he wanted. He was psychologically ready to take his part in the Revolution. Of the broad purposes, the philosophical and political theories, of the revolutionary leaders in the cities, he neither knew nor cared to know anything. All he wanted was the land, and he was ready to help the devil himself in order to get it.

The growth of the economic incentive is not essentially

different in other cases. A wider perspective, a more far-reaching series of calculations, are involved in the other forms of the incentive, but the main idea of justifying confiscation on the basis of the utility theory of ownership is common to all of them.

A Russian workingman, cousin of our peasant, was employed in a factory in Moscow. He belonged to a labor union (*sub rosa*). He had taken part in a strike. He read socialist pamphlets. Without being affiliated with any revolutionary movement himself, he knew several workingmen who were, and he was in sympathy with them. His hours of work were long, his pay was small, and the conditions under which he worked and lived were bad. Still he had a much more interesting and varied life than his cousin the peasant. He was better educated; he could read and write. He took a newspaper and knew in a vague and hazy way something of what was going on in the country. He was thoroughly familiar with the peasant belief that the grand dukes and other aristocrats were robbers, holding land which by right belonged to the peasants. Indeed, his father had come to Moscow from a peasant village not so many years before, and he had a host of relatives who were peasants whom he visited from time to time. He believed, as much as if he were a peasant, that the peasants should own the land, and he inevitably applied the peasant idea of land ownership to the factory in which he worked. The two cases seemed to him to be much alike. None of the owners of the factory worked in it. Even the manager was just a hired man. The owners got a great deal of money every year from his labor and that of his fellow-workmen—none of whom owned any of the factory. It seemed to him that the factory should belong to the man who worked in it and made it produce goods. Of the financial end of the business, of bank loans and credits, of the complicated operations of the purchasing and sales departments, he saw nothing and knew next to nothing. He did not think they were very important. He thought that the man who worked in the factory did all the labor of producing the goods. He knew, indeed, that the factory had to have a manager, but the present manager, or some other, could manage for him and the other workers as easily as for the absent owners. These absent owners were robbers of the workers. He had no sympathy with them. He hated them. He had never seen one of them, but he knew they lived comfortably on the product of his labor. They had no connection with the factory, except to take all the profit it made. The factory and the profit it made should belong to the men who worked in it and made it productive. This idea became as firmly fixed in his mind as the similar idea about land in the mind of his peasant cousin. The absent owners never thought of presenting their side of the case to him—a mere workingman! So they held possession of the factory by mere legal title. He was eager to seize "his" factory and to dispossess the robber owners. He knew that the great Prince Peter Kropotkin believed as he did about the factory and the land. He told his cousin how the Czar had put the Prince in prison and how the Prince had escaped. Perhaps some day, with the help of the Prince and the other sympathetic great ones, he could get possession of the factory. Only the soldiers of the Czar prevented him. If those soldiers could by any means be kept away he could do it, and he was eager for the chance to do it. If he and his fellow-workmen could once get hold of the factory, they would have short hours and good pay and would be comfortable and happy.

It is very easy to point out the crudity, the simplicity,

and the impracticability of such ideas. The important point is that these ideas, or others very like them, did actually develop in the minds of millions of Russian workingmen during the two or three generations before the Revolution. The workingmen in the cities, like the peasants in the country, were psychologically ready for the Revolution. Indeed, the workingmen were better prepared; they were better educated and more alert mentally. City life had freed them from many of the superstitions and traditions which held back the peasants. When, therefore, bold and capable revolutionary leaders pointed out to the city workers how by organizing soviets and going on a general strike, they could render the soldiers helpless and thus get possession of the factories they so eagerly desired, the workingmen were fully prepared and eager to play their part.

In the period preceding the French Revolution the peasants developed the same "hunger for land" which has been noted in Russia. The mental process was essentially the same, and by 1789 the enormous mass of the peasants were ready and eager to confiscate the estates of the nobles and the church. They felt perfectly justified on the basis of their utility theory of property.

The French bourgeoisie present the same phenomenon in a slightly different aspect. In their case it was property right in government which was the issue. These people, the bankers, the merchants, the trades people, and the business class generally were the prime movers in the Revolution. The economic incentive in their case took the form of a desire to get control of the government and the law, particularly the administrative positions, with the idea of using such control for the furthering of their business enterprises. Authority under the ancient régime was in the hands of aristocrats who felt only contempt for the commercial classes. These aristocrats neither knew nor cared anything about business enterprise. As a result, French trade and commerce were being hampered by all sorts of obsolete internal tariffs, customs duties, regulations, rules, and restrictions which were at once burdensome and absurd. A total reconstruction of the system of government and law was necessary if the commercial development of the country was not to be strangled. The enormous sums of public money squandered on mistresses and palaces were needed for roads and bridges, docks and harbors, and a hundred other public improvements essential to the prosperity of the business class.

The French bourgeoisie did not promote the Revolution from any desire to confiscate property. On the contrary, they were believers in the "sacredness" of property. They consented to the confiscation of the lands of the nobles and the church but only to gain the support of the peasants, without which any revolution must have been a failure. Neither did the bourgeoisie, for the most part, expect to make any money directly by gaining control of the government. What they wanted was to get the management of public affairs and the control of public expenditure in their hands, so that they could use these agencies to promote private business enterprise. They were quite sure of their ability to make plenty of money, if only the government and the law were so administered as to be a help instead of a hindrance to private business. They had an indirect, but quite real and urgent, financial interest in overthrowing the old order. The old order prevented them in a thousand ways from getting rich by their own efforts in trade and commerce, so they hated it with a deadly hatred. They were as willing to bring on the Revolution for their own financial reasons as the peasants were in order to get the land.

It is to be noted that the Industrial Revolution had not made any appreciable progress in France up to 1789. There was little large-scale manufacturing. The modern factory-worker had not yet appeared. The city workers were still in the stage of handicraft production. They were without any organization for their own economic betterment, and they gained little or nothing financially from the great Revolution.

The economic incentive to revolution in the case of the American colonists was practically identical with the one which motivated the French bourgeoisie. In the theory of that time, colonies existed only for the benefit of the mother-country. They were not to be allowed to engage in any industry or commerce except such as might tend to the aggrandizement of the parent-state. The British Parliament was supreme over the colonies, and acted on the colonial theory current at the time. No goods could be imported into the colonies, or exported from them, except in British ships Tobacco, turpentine, and other principal colonial products could be shipped to no country except Great Britain. Various kinds of manufactures were interfered with whenever such manufactures seemed to threaten the home trade. These restrictions were so burdensome that many persons of the first importance in society engaged in smuggling, which was very common. It is noteworthy that several such smugglers became prominent revolutionists. Samuel Adams was one; John Hancock, another.

Under such circumstances it was natural that the business men of the American colonies should wish to be free from British rule—and most Americans had a great deal of the business man in their makeup. What they resented, far more than stamp taxes or a duty on tea, was the fact that their financial welfare was always subordinated to that of English business men. The uncertainty of their position angered them. They could never be sure that a carefully built-up business would not be wiped out overnight by the act of a Parliament three thousand miles away. If they only had the government entirely in their own hands, all this vexation and uncertainty would be done away with and a thousand avenues to wealth, closed under colonial government, would open to them. In short, they had the strongest and most imperative economic incentive to revolution.

The economic incentive which drove the English Puritans to revolution had both a positive and a negative aspect. During the period preceding the Revolution, the English middle class were not only well to do, but were daily increasing in prosperity. They were making great improvements in banking methods, commercial organization, shipping, navigation, colonies, fisheries, and the technique of foreign trade. Every such improvement increased their wealth. But the government hindered them in innumerable ways. Usury laws, burdensome duties, monopolies given to court favorites, interference with the right of free contract—all of these things, and many others like them, hindered the middle class in making money. They did make money in spite of all their hindrances, but they were acutely aware that they could make much more money if these hindrances were removed. Then there was a greater danger in prospect. The Stuart kings had inherited a strongly autocratic monarchy from the Tudors. They were striving to make this autocracy absolute. If they succeeded, as appeared not improbable, every man's property would be at the king's mercy. The king openly proclaimed that it was, or should be, at his disposal. Already he was levying tonnage, poundage, customs duties of various kinds, benevolences, forced loans, and other taxes without consent of Parliament. The amount so raised was not excessive but the principle was exceedingly dangerous. Richelieu had already succeeded in making the French monarchy a despotism, and the English monarchy was apparently headed in the same direction.

So the English middle class were inspired by fear, the most potent form of fear to a commercial class—the fear of unlimited future raids on their pocket-books by an absolute monarch. They were thus driven to revolution by the two most compelling of economic incentives—the prospect of great gain and the fear of great loss. Without disparaging in any way the strong religious motives which animated the Puritans, it may be stated that the great struggle of Parliament against king was a pecuniary, as much as a religious, conflict.

The great point of contrast between the French and English revolutions is in the matter of peasant participation. The peasants were an extremely important factor in the French Revolution. It was their revolutionary spirit which made that Revolution a success. In the Puritan Revolution the peasants scarcely appear at all. It was strictly a struggle between the king and the middle class. The reasons for this are too numerous to give in detail. The mass of the English peasants were mere agricultural day laborers, ignorant and poor. There was no great class of independent, landowning peasants such as formed the backbone of the Revolution in France. Then the English landlords, unlike their French compeers, lived on their estates. They knew their peasants personally and, on the whole, were kindly and considerate masters. In times of distress they were liberal in their charities to the unfortunate. Then the great growth of industry and commerce which marked the period opened up many opportunities for employment in the cities, and the English peasant was free to leave the land if he thought he saw an opportunity to better his condition. The English peasant was poor but he was not harassed and irritated by the *gabelle*, the *taille*, and the numerous other feudal dues which so embittered the peasants of France. From such causes as these, it came about that the English peasants took almost no part in the Puritan Revolution. They hated both the royal and parliamentary military forces as thieves, marauders, and disturbers of the countryside. They showed their hatred, where they could, by impartially clubbing to death on the field of battle the wounded soldiers of both armies indiscriminately.

The workingmen in the cities for the most part sided with the Parliament and served in its armies. But the Industrial Revolution was still in the future. The city workers were without effective organization or group coherence. They hardly appear as an independent factor in the situation. Neither they nor the peasants gained any economic advantage from the Revolution.

There were two classes of people more directly concerned in bringing about the Protestant Reformation. One class comprised the kings and nobles, the other was the rising commercial and business order—the middle class. Both classes had powerful economic incentives urging them toward a religious revolution. The zeal of those reformers who were interested in a purely religious change would have effected little, as society was then organized, if the economic necessities of the aristocratic and commercial classes had not caused them to support the Reformation. The ancient church was rich and weak. The kings and lords were poor and powerful. The Renaissance and the maritime discoveries had combined to raise the standard of living of the aristocratic class. They were in desperate need of increased wealth in order to maintain the higher standard of living made imperative by changes in the canons of taste. The church owned enormous landed estates. In many cases these estates amounted to a quarter or a third of all the land in the nation. The income from these great estates was increased by tithes from all secular land and by numerous other fees, taxes, and dues. The total church revenue was far greater than was necessary for the proper support of public worship, and the surplus was expended upon extravagant episcopal and abbatial palaces, magnificent equipages, gold plate, jewels, and other luxuries. The wealth and splendor of the higher clergy were equaled only by their haughtiness and insolence. They were heartily hated by the lay lords whom they quite outdistanced in their style of living. It is little wonder that the secular nobles—poor, proud, and warlike—felt an intense desire to get their hands on the riches of these ecclesiastics. When a religious reform was proposed, which would enable them to better their financial condition at the expense of these hated prelates, they were impelled by a peculiarly keen, economic incentive to regard such a religious reform with the utmost favor.

The kings were in an even worse pecuniary condition than their nobles. The political, social, and economic changes at the beginning of the sixteenth century added greatly to the expenses of government, without bringing in, immediately, any revenue of compensating size. Military and naval forces were much more expensive now that cannon

and gunpowder were the order of the day. The old feudal
levy was useless, and no revenue was at hand to pay for the
newer forms of armament. Moreover, it was now socially
imperative for a king to build new and expensive palaces in
the Italian style, adorned with marbles, tapestries, great
paintings in oil, and other equipment which cost extravagant
sums. Where was a king to get the money to meet the increased cost of government and to maintain this new, expensive style of regal living? He could not tax his secular nobility. They, as a class, were poor; they were in similar financial
straits to himself. In any case, no king in the early part of
the sixteenth century dared to arouse the united antagonism
of an order of men that included all the military leaders in
the country. The middle class were beginning to accumulate
wealth, but they were neither numerous enough nor rich
enough, as yet, to pay taxes at all commensurate to the royal
needs. The peasants were so poor already that little or nothing more could be squeezed out of them. There remained the
church. It was rich. It was almost the only institution of
that age which was rich. It was also corrupt and unpopular.
It sent large sums of money out of the country every year to
Rome—larger sums than found their way into the royal
treasury. Every king hated the thought of all that money
leaving his kingdom. Then the king heard of certain theologians who taught that this enormously rich and expensive
Roman church was not the true Church of Christ at all.
These theologians contended that no money should be sent
to Rome. It was the king's bounden duty, they said, to establish a simple and inexpensive kind of worship and to confiscate all the enormous wealth of the Roman church and apply that wealth to the needs of the government. It sounded
too good to be true. All the kings—Henry VIII, James V,

Gustavus I, Christian III, and Frederick I, not to mention others—sent for the new theologians. Never were any theologians received at court with such honor. Never did kings listen so eagerly to theological doctrines. Was it any wonder? Here was a king in desperate financial difficulties. By a miracle, as it seemed, the way out of his difficulties, the way to greater wealth and affluence than any of his predecessors had ever enjoyed, was presented to him. It was presented to him as his moral and religious duty. It is true he was still somewhat afraid of the pope. But if his warlike nobles were solidly behind him he could brave the papal thunder. It would be necessary to give the nobles a goodly share of the church property, but there was enough for both parties. This is a somewhat simplified but not essentially inaccurate statement of how the economic incentive to religious revolution influenced the kings of England, Scotland, Sweden, Norway, Denmark, and numerous other sovereigns who became Protestants.

The economic incentive which impelled the business men to promote the Protestant Reformation was more important and far reaching than the incentive of the kings and lords. Except in the cities of Northern Italy the business men were not then either very numerous or very powerful. They were increasing in wealth and power but they were very far from being what they are today—the most powerful class in society. They were greatly hindered by lack of investment capital. Commercial opportunities were opening up on all sides. Trade with Asia, America, Africa, and Russia was immensely profitable. But much capital was needed to build and equip the larger and stronger ships required for this transoceanic trade. New docks were necessary for these new ships, and warehouses for the goods they carried. Business was being developed on a much larger scale than in earlier times, and the amount of money necessary to finance it was far larger than the business men could raise from their own resources. It was imperative that the money be obtained from the general public, who were not business men, but who had money that might be invested in business enterprises. The commercial opportunities were such that the business men could well afford to pay a good rate of interest on the money they needed. They were ready and eager to pay such interest. But right here was the rub. Lending money at interest and paying interest on borrowed money were prohibited by the Catholic church. It was the sin of usury., It was not only contrary to law, it was contrary to the moral ideas of the time, which were the result of that church's teaching. The first law legalizing interest on money in England was passed in 1546—the year before the death of Henry VIII. It is true that the legal and moral prohibitions against usury were somewhat largely evaded. But the evaders had an uneasy conscience and a feeling of being engaged in a dirty, underhanded practice. Such was the situation in the period immediately preceding the Reformation: magnificent commercial opportunities; a growing class of capable business men, eager to take advantage of these opportunities and abundantly able to do so if only they could get the necessary capital; a public with funds ready for investment; a church which prohibited the giving and receiving of interest on money.

Then the business men heard of the new theologians who were opposing the ancient church. The business men cared little about most theological doctrines, but there was one theological doctrine they did care very much about. They sent delegations to the theologians—important delegations of wealthy business men. The theologians received numerous letters from business men in many cities. What was the teaching of the Protestants about interest on money?[1] John Calvin gave the answer. He was a statesman as well as a theologian. He realized that the business men were becoming a power in the world. Their conversion to the new faith would be of the utmost advantage. When the delegation of important business men asked him about interest on money, he promulgated the doctrine which now rules the world. That doctrine is that there is a distinction between "usury" and "interest." Usury is excessive interest and is immoral. But the sin is in the excessiveness of the rate. Interest, in itself, is moral, if it is not excessive—if it does not exceed, say, 8 or 10 per cent. So said John Calvin. According to the old Catholic doctrine, there was no more ethical difference between 5 per cent interest and 50 per cent interest than there was between stealing five dollars and stealing fifty dollars. The sin was in interest as such, irrespective of the amount involved.

John Calvin was a great man. He founded the Presbyterian church. Millions of business men are devoted members of that church. It is right that they should be. Incidentally, the confiscation of the wealth of the Catholic church released large sums of money which furnished Calvin's business men with much of the capital they needed. The reduction of the inordinate number of church holidays which had existed under Catholicism greatly aided economic production. Money formerly spent on cathedrals and abbeys was put into business enterprises. But the moralizing of investment funds was the essential thing. It was the economic incentive which drove the business men to support re-

[1] R. Tawney, *Religion and the Rise of Capitalism*, chap. ii.

ligious reformation. John Calvin is more than the theological father of Presbyterianism; he is the theological father of modern capitalism. All churches, Catholic and Protestant, have accepted his doctrine of interest on money.[1]

The greatest of all religious revolutions, that known as the "Conversion of the Roman Empire" to Christianity, had its economic incentive. It was probably, as a whole, the most idealistic and least selfish revolution in world-history. It triumphed largely by spiritual appeal, but not entirely by spiritual appeal. It was a regular practice of the great Christian leaders of the early centuries to add also an economic appeal—an appeal directed intentionally to the pecuniary interests of the masses of the people to whom they preached. They emphasized the gross inequality of wealth which then prevailed. They drew attention to the exploitation suffered by the poorer classes. They assured their hearers that these injustices would be remedied in the day of Christian victory over paganism. They were more especially vehement in denouncing the holders of great wealth, who lived in luxury and did little or nothing for the benefit of society. They insisted that such wealth belonged to the poor. They advocated the confiscation of the huge endowments of the pagan temples and the use of this property for purposes of the common welfare. They pictured in vivid colors the benefits which would accrue to the masses of the people from such expropriation.

Moreover, the early Christians were extremely charitable. They did their utmost for the poor and needy, especially

[1] Max Weber, in his *Religions soziologie*, points out the intimate connection between modern capitalistic ideology and the doctrines of Calvinism. He would reverse the Marxian dictum that religious attitudes are rooted in the economic system to read: "The system of production grows out of the dominant attitudes."

those who were members of the church. Very many thousands of people in the lower ranks of society were influenced to profess the Christian faith by the knowledge that, if they became Christians, the church members could be depended upon to take care of them in case they met with misfortune and needed help.

There was another economic incentive which made innumerable converts to Christianity in its early period. This incentive was of a very strange sort. It seems incredibly weird and fantastic to us today, but it was a most powerful incentive at the time. It was the "millennial hope." The earlier generations of Christians believed that the second coming of Christ was very near at hand. It might happen any time, and was certain to happen before very long. This second coming of the Lord was to be quite unlike the first. Christ was to return in power and great glory. He was to reign in Jerusalem as ruler over the whole world. The Roman Empire was to be miraculously destroyed along with all other earthly governments. The saints, i.e., the Christians, were to reign with Christ over a totally renovated world wherein was no suffering or disease and when the ground would yield fruits in incredible abundance. Some of the accounts of this abundance surpass fairy tales. One writer describes grapevines: Each vine was to have a thousand branches, each branch a thousand clusters, and each cluster a thousand grapes.

Wild as such beliefs may appear, there is most indubitable evidence that they were widely preached, that they were highly popular, that they were devoutly believed, and that they influenced very great numbers of people to embrace Christianity. The frequency with which these beliefs appear in the early Christian writings will astonish anyone

not familiar with that literature. Such beliefs were eminently qualified to appeal to ignorant, poor, and superstitious
people such as formed the lower classes of the great Mediterranean cities. It was precisely among the populace of these
cities that Christianity made its first great gains. The prospect of the more or less immediate enjoyment of incredible
luxury and power, without making any effort and as the result simply of professing Christianity and joining the church
—this was undoubtedly an economic incentive of enormous
power. The very crude and direct manner in which this incentive was employed, by at least a great number of the
early Christian missionaries, astonishes anyone not ac-
quainted with the ideas of that age.

It would be totally false to give the impression that early
Christian evangelism contained nothing but this wild fanta-
sy. It inculcated the purest morality and the most unselfish
conduct, but the millennial hope was still there.

The millennial hope of the early Christians may serve as
an introduction to the second master-symptom of revolution.
A master-symptom is one which, in a marked degree, conditions others and without which a great revolution is impossible. According to this analysis, two master-symptoms
appear in pre-revolutionary society. One is the "transfer of
the allegiance of the intellectuals"; the other is the "social
myth." It is a comment on the essentially mystic character
of the human race that even extreme discontent with existing
conditions, though voiced by most eloquent publicists and
reinforced by the strongest economic incentives, never, of
itself, produces a real revolution. If such a revolution is to
eventuate, a dynamic of a genuinely spiritual and religious
kind is absolutely necessary. Le Bon has shown that all
great revolutions have this essentially religious element.

Without a super-rational "theological" dynamic no great revolution is possible—at any rate, none has ever occurred. It would even seem that a revolution is only great and important in the degree to which this element is present. All great revolutions are "religious" revolutions in the original, etymological sense of the word. They are carried through by men who feel themselves to be, in a special manner, "tied" or "bound" to "God," the "Universe," or the "Ultimate Power" conceived in some fashion.

The French philosopher Sorel named this spiritual dynamic of revolution the "social myth." The social myth arises from a fusion of the ideas propounded by the revolutionary intellectuals with the elemental wishes of the repressed class of the society concerned. Out of the innumerable criticisms of "things as they are" and the equally innumerable hopes of "things as they might be" there gradually emerges a new ideal. This ideal is all embracing. It includes in a new totality the strongest as well as the weakest inclinations and desires of the discontented, repressed class. It so frames an indeterminate future as to give an aspect of complete reality to the hopes of the present. Psychologically, it is "a new heaven and a new earth." It is able to effect a complete transformation of the desires, passions, and ideas of those who accept it. It is the most powerful dynamic force which operates in human society, with the two exceptions of hunger and sexual love. It can make the miser a generous man and the generous man a miser. It can change a cruel man into a humanitarian and a humane man into a monster of cruelty. It is the power commonly spoken of as "religious conversion" or the "power of salvation." The social myth is the power of salvation generalized to include many phenomena not commonly spoken of as religious.

Every social myth contains elements which, considered from a rational viewpoint, are mutually inconsistent and contradictory. Many of them are incapable of verification by experience. The whole social myth may be entirely delusional. Such objections are of no importance. The power of the myth comes not from itself but from the intensity of the faith with which it is believed.

It would seem that, in order to carry out any social task of especially great difficulty and danger, a group must be in some way spiritually strengthened or reinforced in morale. It must be made to feel that it is "carrying out the will of God," "altering the course of history," "co-operating with the forces of evolution," or something of a like transcendental sort. The social myth is essentially super-, or, possibly, subrational—perhaps both. It is not susceptible of demonstration by ordinary methods of proof. It is faith, not reason. "This is the victory which overcometh the world," said the Apostle, "even our faith." The history of every great revolution is a commentary upon that text.

The social myth of the early Christians was the second coming of Christ and the reign of the saints in the new Jerusalem. The second coming of Christ never took place, and the reign of the saints was a delusion. Yet faith in these things converted millions of people. It enabled thousands of martyrs to endure the most excruciating tortures with expressions of joy upon their faces and words of happiness upon their lips. It overthrew an ancient and widespread system of religion, backed by all the physical force of a world-empire. It changed a poor, despised Jewish sect into the most powerful theocracy in history. This faith may be considered totally absurd. Yet without it Christianity would have had no history—no existence.

The great Protestant reformers—Luther, Calvin, Knox, and the others—established new theological systems. They taught that eternal salvation depended upon "justification by faith," "predestination," "election," and similar things. Whether this is true or not cannot be discovered by reason. In the eyes of rational logic, predestination, for instance, is a perfect example of an irreconcilable contradiction. It would seem impossible to base a system of morality upon it. According to this doctrine God consigns men before birth either to salvation or damnation. Nothing they do while alive will change this fate. They should, logically, indulge themselves without limit. Yet Presbyterians were and are honorably distinguished for pureness of life. Calvin had no difficulty in erecting a most severe morality upon a totally illogical basis.

Whatever may be thought of Protestant theology, it is certain that Protestant theology changed the face of Europe. It abolished political, social, and economic institutions which had governed the peoples of the Western civilization for centuries. It "altered the course of history." It was a social myth.

The English Puritans, somewhat like the early Christians, were going to have a "reign of the saints"—they being the "saints." Some of them even revived the millennial hope. They had a great ideal. It was to establish a theocracy in which the Bible was to be the fundamental law, and only "pious and godly" men were to hold any office of power or honor. All profane amusements such as theaters, dances, and Christmas celebrations were to be abolished. No light, vain, or frivolous conduct was to be allowed. The Puritans sincerely believed themselves to be the chosen people of God. They were convinced that they were especially "well pleasing in His sight." They were "called" to do "His will," and they were under immediate, divine guidance in doing it. No political, legal, or social institution was allowed by them to stand in the way of carrying out the divine will ascertained directly from the Deity in answer to prayer.

Whatever may be thought of these beliefs they were the power which, operating through the famous "new model" army, overthrew both the monarchy and the Parliament. These beliefs were the dynamic which founded New England and ruled Old England. The Puritans, inspired by these beliefs, conquered Ireland and drenched it in Catholic blood. They subdued Scotland. They humbled Spain and Holland. Even the Algerine pirates stood in awe of them. The very pope trembled lest Puritan fanaticism, in control of the most powerful navy in the world, should send a fleet to the Tiber to knock the city of Rome about his ears. Bloody bigot though he was, Alexander VII ceased to persecute the Protestants of Piedmont when the Puritan battleships entered the Mediterranean.

It is impossible to know by reason whether or not the Puritans were the chosen people of God. It is certain that, except for their firm belief that they were the chosen people, such a small sect, numbering less than a tenth of the population of England, could never have done such extraordinary and nearly incredible things. To an almost miraculous degree the "reign of the saints" became a reality, because it was fanatically believed in. It was a social myth.

The social myth which animated the American revolutionists has become a reality. It was the ideal of a great, powerful, wealthy, independent, and united nation, free and respected by all the world—"able to lick any country on the map with one hand." The old-fashioned Fourth of July oration, wherein the Stars and Stripes waved, the Eagle screamed, and the Lion's tail was twisted, represented very closely the social myth of the "Founding Fathers." Without the inspiration of that ideal, the revolutionary troops could never have survived the long agony of Valley Forge or the numerous defeats preceding it.

The social myth of the French Revolution is still to be seen epitomized in the three words engraved on the public buildings of France: *Liberté, Egalité, Fraternité*. Enthusiasm for the principles embodied in these three words swept over France like a new religion. The French revolutionists felt that they were the apostles of a new faith which was destined to regenerate the world. This belief enabled the tatterdemalion French troops, often hungry and barefooted, to triumph over the most-experienced and best-equipped armies of Europe. Like all apostles, they were eager to sacrifice themselves for their belief, which, according to their dreams, was to renew the world. The political leaders—Marat, St. Just, Robespierre, and the rest—had the same mystic mentality. Persuaded that their magnificent formula could overturn all the thrones, they dreamed of converting the globe. As strong faith is always superior to weak or doubtful faith, they were victorious against the coalition of all Europe. They did not accomplish all that they dreamed, but without their dream they could have accomplished nothing.

Exactly the same thing is true of the Russian Revolution. The great red leaders—Lenin, Trotsky, Kalenin, and others—are not to be thought of as ordinary statesmen or politicians, governed by the usual motives of gain or expediency. Essentially they were evangelists preaching the gospel of St. Marx. Communism was the new religion which was to save the world. *Das Kapital* was its Bible. The armies of the soviet were commanded by men greatly deficient in military training and experience. The soldiers were poorly equipped. But officers and men alike burned with a fiery zeal for their belief. They easily defeated the highly trained and perfectly equipped armies sent against them by the United States, Great Britain, France, and many other nations. Their victory was due to spiritual not physical causes. The enemy armies were only soldiers fighting a war they but half believed in. The soviet armies were apostles going forth to battle for their faith. It was their social myth which gave them victory.

SELECTED REFERENCES

CAMBRIDGE. *Modern History*, Vol. VIII, chaps. ii and viii. Vol. II, chap. xiv; New York and London, 1902–12.

EDWARDS, LYFORD P. *The Transformation of Early Christianity* (from an eschatological to a socialized movement), chap. ii. Menasha, Wis., 1919.

GARDINER, SAMUEL RAWSON. *History of England* (from the accession of James I to the outbreak of the Civil War, 1603–42), Vol. IX. London and New York, 1884–91.

HAYES, CARLETON J. H. *A Political and Social History of Modern Europe*, Vol. I, chap. iv. New York, 1916.

HYNDMAN, HENRY MAYERS. *The Evolution of Revolution*, chap. xxi. London, 1921.

KAUTSKY, KARL. *The Social Revolution*. Chicago, 1903.

KROPOTKIN, PETER A. *Fields, Factories, and Workshops: or Industry Combined with Agriculture and Brain Work with Manual Work*. London, 1919.

LANDAUER, GUSTAV. *Die Revolution*. Frankfort-on-the-Main, 1923.

LE BON, GUSTAVE. *The Psychology of Revolution*. New York, 1913.
———. *The Psychology of Socialism*. New York, 1899.

MAVOR, JAMES. *An Economic History of Russia*, Vol. II, Book V, chap. vii. London, 1925.

READE, WILLIAM HENRY VINCENT. *The Revolt of Labour against Civilisation*. New York, 1919.

ROSS, EDWARD A. *Russia in Upheaval*, chap. vii. New York, 1918.

SCHLESINGER, ARTHUR MEIER. *New Viewpoints in American History*, chap. vii. New York, 1922.

SOREL, GEORGES. *Reflections on Violence*. New York, 1914.

STODDARD, THEODORE LOTHROP. *The Revolt against Civilization; the Menace of the Underman*. New York, 1922.

TAWNEY, RICHARD H. *The Acquisitive Society*. New York, 1920.

———. *Religion and the Rise of Capitalism*, chap. ii. New York, 1926.

TREVELYAN, GEORGE MACAULAY. *England under the Stuarts* (12th ed.), chap. x. London, 1925.

WEBER, MAX. *Religionssoziologie*, Vol. I. Tübingen, 1922.

CHAPTER VI

THE OUTBREAK OF REVOLUTION

The outbreak of revolution is commonly signaled by some act, insignificant in itself, which precipitates a separation of the repressors and their followers from the repressed and their followers. The St. Petersburg strike in February, 1917; the Boston Tea Party; the storming of the Bastile; the attempt on the five members; and Luther's burning of the papal bull are illustrations. The historical importance of such events is great, but it comes entirely from the social cleavage which they reveal. The cleavage was there, but its existence was not acknowledged—at least, explicitly. When the time comes that the social cleavage is accomplished, almost any event may serve to bring it to light. The happening which "starts off" a revolution is generally, perhaps always, so much like similar acts which have preceded it that it can be identified only by what follows it. Its true character cannot be recognized on the day it occurs. Nevertheless, it has one distinguishing mark: It is a true precipitate; that is to say, it is a really illegal and revolutionary act clearly recognizable as such. But this is not enough to isolate it. Equally illegal and revolutionary acts, clearly recognizable as such, happen numbers of times in every pre-revolutionary society. Some of them are of far more importance per se than the act which starts the revolution. Yet they are of small significance because they occur before the psychological preparation for revolution is complete. The act which starts a revolution is that one of a series of lawless actions

98

which coincides with the completion of the psychological preparation for revolution.

The mental and emotional preparation for revolution is only complete when any casual crowd of members of the repressed class can be depended upon to act in a revolutionary capacity consistently and over a long period of time. All revolutionary factors are of slow development, but the revolutionary mob is slowest of all. Perhaps no current opinion is more erroneous than the notion that the actions of mobs are sudden and unpredictable. In its range of action and its methods of action a mob is more rigidly circumscribed than almost any other human group. A crowd is open to suggestions that are in line with its previous experiences—and to no others. Any suggestion out of line with a crowd's previous experience immediately disintegrates it. Ancient Jewish mobs always stoned their victims to death, Alexandrian mobs nearly always threw theirs from the tops of high buildings—Hypatia is almost the only exception. She was cut to pieces with oyster shells. Medieval mobs regularly decapitated those they killed. Except in unusual circumstances American mobs use the noose. A Belfast mob could no more be brought to lynch negroes than a Chicago mob could be brought to lynch Catholics. An Odessa mob will lynch Jews, not negroes or Catholics.

The main characteristics of crowd psychology are familiar enough. Crowds do not reason. They accept or reject ideas as a whole. They are governed by phrases, symbols, and shibboleths. They tolerate neither discussion nor contradiction. The suggestions brought to bear on them invade the whole of their understanding and tend to transform themselves at once into acts. Crowds entertain only violent and extreme sentiments, and they accord a mysterious power to the leader or the formula which has aroused their enthusiasm. Any movement in order to become popular, in order to "get over" to the crowd, must operate within the limits set by this psychology. The amount of change, adaptation, and development which must take place in the revolutionary movement itself, and in the experience of the members of the public, before a revolutionary mob can be formed is very great—so great that decades and generations are required for it. It took something more than a hundred and fifty years to change the Alexandrian populace from a pagan mob that lynched Christians into a Christian mob that lynched pagans. It took considerably longer to change the London crowd from Catholics who mobbed Protestants into Protestants who mobbed Catholics. It is possible to change a violently monarchical mob into a violently republican one, but it is an exceedingly slow and difficult thing to do. It is much slower and more difficult than converting an equal number of individuals separately.

In the progress from one extreme to the other a dead center is reached where the mob halts between two opinions; becomes powerless and does nothing. At such times a government which knows its own mind is practically absolute—it has no effective public in opposition. Such was the government of Henry VIII in his later days. England had ceased to be papal but had not become Protestant. Henry VIII was able to burn both convinced Romanists and convinced Protestants on the same day in the same fire.

There is much popular exaggeration of the rôle of mobs in revolution. Mobs do play an essential part in certain revolutionary crises, but these crises are few and in some important revolutions they never occur at all. Even in the French Revolution, where mob action was most conspicuous, it played a decisive part only on five or six days during more than that number of years. In the Russian Revolution the mob was of importance only twice—in February and October of 1917. In the American Revolution mobs were never a decisive factor. The same is true of the Puritan Revolution. Only in the easily repressed peasant revolt did the mob figure to any great extent in the Protestant Reformation. Even then the mob had no decisive part in the outcome of the great struggle. In the early Christian Revolution the abasement of Theodosius by the Milanese mob stands almost alone. Athanasius had the Alexandrian and Nitrian mobs at his back but they played no essential part in the drama.

Mob action is thus only occasionally important in some revolutions. When it is decisive, the decisiveness is due entirely to the social situation at the moment and not to anything unusual in the character or actions of the mob concerned. Mobs which intervene decisively at the crises of revolution are always raised and organized for the purpose by a small group of revolutionary leaders acting through subordinates. The mob's activities are carefully planned out beforehand and directed toward the end which the leaders have in view. The whole procedure, so far from being a spontaneous outburst of violence, is the exact opposite. Mob intervention in revolution is never important except when it is thus deliberately organized and used by a directing group. On such occasions mob violence is used simply for strategic purposes or because more effective forces, such as an army movement or a legislative decree, are not available at the moment. Mobs whose actions are decisive in revolutionary crises are always tools.

The idea that revolutionary mobs are more cruel and

bloodthirsty than other mobs is without foundation. So is the idea that mob violence is especially characteristic of revolutionary societies. The truth is rather the reverse. No mob in any revolution perpetrates greater atrocities than are perpetrated by mobs in thoroughly stable and conservative societies. Mobs are fully as characteristic of firmly established "standpatter" groups as of unstable and radical ones. The idea that revolutionary mobs are composed of "the scum" and "the riffraff," of beggars and thugs and thieves, is also mistaken. Such persons may be present but the important part of any mob playing a decisive revolutionary rôle is always made up of decent, self-respecting common people, mechanics and laborers, butchers and bakers and candlestick-makers.

No proletarian mob is more ferocious and bloody minded than another crowd composed of the members of the upper classes of educated, refined people. Any mob will do things both better and worse than any individual in the mob could be persuaded to do when alone. The nature of the mob activity, whether good or bad, is decided by the leadership and the circumstances, not by the social class composing the mob.

Many of these facts are contrary to popular opinion, but a very little study of the history of mobs will abundantly prove their truth. No revolutionary mobs exceed in cruelty the mobs which for many years have held lynchings in a part of the United States where conservatism reigns supreme. In that part of the United States the lynching mobs are not composed only of the scum and the riffraff but of respectable and responsible citizens. The Boston Tea Party was not composed of criminals but of young men of decent, self-respecting families. It included Paul Revere and Dr.

Young. The leader of the mob that stormed the Bastile was a tradesman in a good way of business. The mob included priests and nobles as well as beggars and thieves, but it was mostly made up of decent people of the common class. The Gordon riots were probably the most extensive and most long-continued exhibition of mob violence in English history. They occurred in a peaceful, stable, and conservative society. They did not even threaten the social structure of England in the smallest degree. The leader was the son of a duke, and the danger as well as the importance of this great outbreak was practically nothing. The same is true of most mob activities both in revolutionary and in peaceful societies. The danger to society from mob violence is greatly exaggerated in the popular mind. Scarcely once in a century do mobs get beyond mere popular tumults, proper occasions for the activities of the police, but of no more moment than that.

The performances of revolutionary mobs, being often highly spectacular, have attracted a degree of attention altogether in excess of their importance. On those rare occasions where mob violence is of moment, there is nothing out of the ordinary about the mob itself. The Roman mob in the Flavian amphitheater during the most peaceful era in the world's history shows exactly the same characteristics as the Paris mob in the most violent days of the Terror. Those "very perfect gentle knights," the Comte de Foix and the Captal de Buch and the aristocratic crowd they led, were fully as brutal and ferocious as any mob of serfs and peasants in the Jacquerie. The infamous cruelty of the Landgrave of Hesse and the German nobles in the *Bauern Krieg* equaled and surpassed that of the peasant mobs. All sorts of mobs—Christian and pagan,

Jew and Gentile, Catholic and Protestant, Republican and Royalist, aristocrat and proletarian—present identically the same psychology. There is nothing to choose between wartime mobs and peacetime mobs, revolutionary mobs and anti-revolutionary mobs, high-brow mobs or low-brow mobs. They are all alike in their behavior patterns, and in the methods by which they are influenced.

An understanding of the uniformity and insignificance of mobs is necessary if one wishes to get a rational and scientific knowledge of revolutions instead of an emotional and sentimental impression of them. Mob violence presents literature with a most dramatic theme, as all readers of Hugo and Dickens can attest. But the importance of mob violence as a literary theme is equaled only by its unimportance as a form of social action.

A mob is nothing but an ordinary crowd in action. The particular mob action which generally starts a revolution meets with practically unanimous acceptance from the society concerned in spite of the fact that it reveals a cleavage in that society. This is due to the fact that everybody, except the few reactionaries, agrees that reform must come, and almost nobody realizes that it is revolution instead of reform that is coming. This opening act of revolution also gains popular support because there generally is at the time some special cause of discontent. Quite commonly this is a shortage of food. Many of the mob that stormed the Bastile were hungry. The day before they took the Bastile they sacked the convent of the Lazarites and confiscated more than fifty cartloads of wheat for food. The French harvests of 1788 and 1789 were bad, and there was acute suffering among the poor.

The same was true in Russia in 1917. Great "bread

lines" numbering into the thousands were to be seen lined up at every relief station in the large cities during the weeks preceding the outbreak of the revolution. Bread riots disturbed the whole city of St. Petersburg on March 8 only two days before the czarist government was overthrown.

A similar food shortage marks the outbreak of the German *Bauern Krieg* in 1524. In the outbreaks at the beginning of the Puritan and American revolutions the special circumstances were not food shortages but particular despotic acts of the rulers—the attempts to seize the five members of Parliament and the attempt to exact a duty on tea. The particular circumstances that thus incite the first revolutionary outbreak are not of great moment and would not ordinarily provoke any serious consequences. The outbreak of revolution is never due to any one cause. It is due to a complicated accumulation of stresses, to a multiplication of nervous tensions, to a concurrence of provocations, any one of which by itself would be of little moment.

There is one important reason why some quite ordinary act of mob violence generally proves to be the start of revolution. It is helpless incompetence revealed by the governing class in the emergency. This incompetence has long been a fact, but it is advertised in a particularly spectacular way by the circumstances of the first outbreak. If the commander of the Bastile had not been a spiritless imbecile, the Bastile could never have been captured. Two-thirds of his garrison were more or less in sympathy with the populace. Louis XVI was repeatedly urged to replace De Launey with a competent commander and to man the fortress with reliable troops. Through sheer indolence and indecisiveness he neglected to do either. The grotesque blunderings and stupidities of which Charles I was guilty in his attempt to seize the five members of Parliament not only insured the failure of that criminal action but discouraged all his supporters and encouraged all his enemies. The way the royal government mishandled the Boston Tea Party crisis was almost moronic. There were both military and naval forces available to protect the tea ships amply. No attempt was made to use these forces, though nearly everybody in Boston seems to have been aware that an attempt was to be made to destroy the tea. The incredible folly of the Boston Port Bill and the other legislation with which the British Parliament followed up the Tea Party can only be likened to the pouring of oil on a fire. It changed a small, unimportant blaze into a great, destructive conflagration.

Pope Leo X and the Emperor Charles V handled the religious revolution in a similar bungling manner at its first outbreak in 1520. Bulls and decrees were issued but not carried into effect. Impotence, indecision, and incompetence marked the proceedings of both of the chief enemies of the Reformation. Luther's success in defying at once the papal bull and the decree of the Diet of Worms is really a measure of the incapacity of his opponents. Such a striking exhibition of Catholic imbecility naturally encouraged all the reformers to take still more radical steps.

The czar Nicholas II may not have been an actual mental defective, but his handling of affairs at the outbreak of the revolution in March, 1917, strongly suggests it. In spite of the most urgent representations he kept troops in St. Petersburg who were known to be in sympathy with the people; he refused to appoint a government responsible to the Duma. He let himself get caught and separated from his loyal troops, and he let these troops in turn get caught at an impossible distance from the capital. He left the railroads in control of an official about whose revolutionary leanings he had been repeatedly warned. It is the exhibition of a man trying to rule an empire without brains enough to run a grocery store.

The outbreak of revolution is due as much to this revelation of the inability of the ruling class to handle even an ordinary riot as to anything else. A ruling class which cannot perform even the common duties of police at once reveals itself as impotent. It invites repeated attack and receives it until it is destroyed. This invokes the disintegration of society. But revolution is much more than the disintegration of society. It is at the same time the reintegration of society along different and more efficient lines. A revolution is not a period of anarchy; that is the last thing it is. It is a period of despotism, with instant destruction to everyone opposing that despotism. Caesar and Cromwell, Robespierre and Lenin, were not anarchists; they were autocrats. There is not less government during a revolution, there is more government. Not only are there more laws, but these laws are enforced with a thoroughness quite unknown in ordinary times. The popular superstition that revolution and anarchy are closely synonymous is due to a legal fiction. This legal fiction runs to the effect that sovereign power can only be exercised in specified "legal" ways and by specified "legal" agencies. There is no quarrel with this fiction. It is useful and necessary in peaceable societies. But it is contrary to fact—the fact of revolution. Revolution is the exercise of sovereign power in ways and by agencies not previously specified as "legal." Revolution is not legal in the ordinary sense, though it presently legalizes itself if it is successful. Revolution is not law, but it is in a real sense "superlaw." It is pure sovereignty. It is the will of the people in direct action. As such it is the creator and destroyer of all law and all legality. It is the ultimate source and end of all authority. There is not a government or a law in the world today whose authority and legality are not based ultimately upon the so-called "anarchy" of revolution.

There is a trick of the mind which causes us to project our ideas of legality (and other things) into social situations in which they do not apply. Anarchy and lawlessness are closely associated in peaceable societies. But lawlessness and anarchy are actually two totally different things. Revolutions are lawless until they succeed, but they are never anarchical. There is no lack of order in revolution, no lack of social control. Only the order and control are of a new and different kind—a kind to which the world in general is not accustomed, and which it does not recognize for a while. So it comes about that the lawlessness of peaceable times gets confused with the pure sovereignty of revolution, and the label of anarchy gets pasted on its exact opposite, the autocracy of revolution.

But this confusion is one of thought and names only. The reality remains unaffected, and the reality of revolution is rigid obedience to absolute despotism. The Paris guillotine was perfectly real government. It beheaded those who disobeyed the decrees of the Convention. No French laws have ever been obeyed half so carefully as the decrees of the Convention during the Terror.

Lenin in actual fact was a dictator and ruled Russia with more power than any czar. The dictatorship of the proletariat was a new kind of government, but it was an exceedingly real kind of government. Those who obeyed with entire submission were perfectly safe; those who disobeyed it in the least particular were shot. The reality of revolutionary government is quite unaffected by any obsolescent fiction about its legality.

The primary function of government is that of police, the maintenance of order. As soon as the outbreak of revolution makes it clear that the legal government no longer has the power necessary to perform this primary function, it becomes absolutely essential that some superlegal government be established which does have the necessary power. The need for authority with power is elemental in civilized society. This need is so urgent that it takes precedence of all other needs. So the setting up of an authority with power—the power of police at least—is always and inevitably a part of the outbreak of revolution. It is the essential part. The spectacular attack on the Bastile is the disintegration of society. The unspectacular work of enrolling, equipping, and drilling the "citizen guard" is the reintegration of society.

On the day before the storming of the Bastile the people of Paris assembled in huge crowds at the Hotel de Ville. They at once decided that a citizen guard should be established. Almost every able-bodied man was eager to join the guard for the protection of the city. The number chosen was forty-eight thousand men who were apportioned among the sixty city districts. They were all enrolled in a few hours. A committee was appointed to watch night and day over the safety of the city. The new guards took the oath of fidelity: "To the Assembly of the Citizens." Thus a new and independent government with the power necessary for the police function was established in one day. This government was entirely detached from Louis XVI. It was "illegal," revolutionary—and real.

So Massachusetts and the other American colonies set up

independent governments at the time of the Boston Tea Party and immediately after that event, but before any armed outbreak. A New England Provincial Congress met at Salem. It levied taxes and ordered that these taxes and all others, except local imposts, be paid to a receiver-general appointed by it. This was done. It appointed a Committee of Safety with power to enrol and arm a large force of militia. This Committee did its work with extraordinary thoroughness and rapidity. In a very few days troops were equipped somehow, and were being drilled in every town in the colony. Ammunition and stores were collected at Concord and other places. The supplies of the British troops from the country were cut off. The few colonial or local officials who refused to obey the Congress were ousted by the people and obedient ones substituted. This Provincial Congress was absolutely illegal, but it was the actual government of Massachusetts and it was a despotic government. Anyone who refused obedience to it (and there were several) was mobbed and was lucky to escape with nothing worse than a coat of tar and feathers. The Minute Men who fought at Lexington and Concord were not unorganized anarchists "out on their own hook." They were regularly organized militiamen, armed and equipped by the authority of the Provincial Congress, and they fought under the command of its officers. It is true that the Provincial Congress did not in form declare itself independent of the royal government, but it was independent in fact. While these things were going on in Massachusetts, similar independent governments were being set up in the other colonies. The First Continental Congress was also elected, and within its sphere functioned as an illegal but actual government for the colonies as a whole.

Immediately after the attempt of Charles I to seize the five members, Parliament reorganized the county militia under the command of men devoted to its cause. The House of Commons on its own sole authority voted to appoint new commanders of the three great arsenals of the kingdom: Hull, Portsmouth, and the Tower of London. These new commanders were supplied with troops loyal to the Parliament. The "trained bands" of London were sworn "to defend the Parliament" as were the London watermen—at that time a numerous body. Lord Warwick was put in command of the navy by authority of Parliament, and a large loan was raised by authority of Parliament to meet the expenses involved by these measures. All of this activity, which insured the absolute control by Parliament of the greater part of England, was utterly "illegal" usurpation, but it was none the less effective government for that.

The procedure in the Russian Revolution was so nearly identical that it is needless to give the details, which are recent enough to be remembered by most people. The "bread riots" broke out in St. Petersburg on March 8, 1917. The police fired on the mob, but some of the troops went over to the mob. The radicals in the Duma planned a new government, and within five days the new government was in control of St. Petersburg and Moscow. Just a week from the outbreak of the Revolution the Czar abdicated. The extreme rapidity of events in the Russian Revolution is due to the fact that this Revolution took place in a society equipped with the modern apparatus for rapid communication and transportation. It was not due to any peculiarity in the Revolution itself. The earlier revolutions were more leisurely only because of the relatively imperfect development of the machine technology in those times. Other revolutions of the present day, the German and Austrian for example, were quite as rapid as the Russian.

Coincident with the outbreak of revolution and the organization of revolutionary governments, there is a phenomenon worth notice: It is the enormous development of shibboleths and other isolation devices by which both the disintegration and the reintegration of society become visible to the eye and audible to the ear. A "shibboleth" is a word, a formula, or a symbol which means exactly opposite things to different groups of people. It arouses love and loyalty on one side, anger and hatred on the other. Reaction to it is immediate, unrestrained, and unreasoning. It is, in consequence, capable of unloosing an enormous amount of pent-up emotion, whenever, as in the beginning of a revolution, an enormous amount of pent-up emotion needs to find expression. Shibboleths seem to be developed and adopted almost instantaneously, but this speed is largely a delusion. Any group, before it will adopt a new shibboleth with any degree of enthusiasm, must be subjected to the long, slow process of forming habits of thought in line with the ideas expressed by the shibboleth. The rapid adoption of shibboleths at the outbreak of a revolution is due to the long "campaign of education" carried on by the intellectuals during the years preceding the outbreak. The term "isolation device" is more general than shibboleth. It includes shibboleth and any other means, physical or mental, by which the separation between two or more social groups is accentuated. All conflict groups originate from physical or mental isolation and depend upon it for their survival. The sudden appearance of a great number of isolation devices is a proof that the process of mental isolation has been long under way, and is a sign that a rapid organization of contending factions is taking place.

In the contest between early Christianity and paganism the name Christ and the cross as a gesture or embodied in some material fabric were shibboleths. They aroused passionate loyalty in the Christians and bitter antagonism in the pagans. Isolation devices included the sacraments of baptism, confirmation, and the mass. They all tended to give the Christians a feeling both of solidarity among themselves and of separateness from the unbaptized and unconfirmed pagans who did not have these sacraments or that of the mass. Of course, the pagan religious rituals and the civic and other ceremonies in honor of the Olympian gods were a complementary series of pagan isolation devices.

In the Protestant Reformation the words "Catholic" and "Protestant," "papist" and "heretic," "Romanist" and "Lutheran," "Calvinist," "Anabaptist," "mass," "confession," "monk," "pope," and many others were shibboleths. Isolation devices included religious creeds, church architecture and ritual, speech habits (swearing by saints for Catholics and Bible quotations for Protestants), eating habits (fish on Fridays and Lenten fasts), work habits (Catholic saints' days and other church holidays), dress habits (wearing of crosses, crucifixes, and amulets), and national patriotism (loyalty to the nation identified with adherence to the state religion).

In the Puritan Revolution word shibboleths were "Cavalier" and "Roundhead," "Royalist" and "Parliament man," "prelate" and "Puritan," "Episcopalian" and "Presbyterian." Isolation devices were dress habits (the long, curled hair and elaborate clothes of the Cavalier; the straight hair and sober clothes of the Puritan), speech habits (oaths and free language for the Cavalier; pious phrases and Bible texts with a predominance of nasal sounds for the Puritan), play habits (theaters, dances, gambling, and general liberty or license for the Cavalier; the strict avoidance of all these for the Puritan), and economic habits (carelessness, with extravagance and debt, for the Cavalier; close attention to money matters, thrift, and solvency for the Puritan).

At the opening of the American Revolution the shibboleths that appeared included several kinds of flags: the pine-tree flag, the liberty-tree flag, the coiled-snake flag in several designs, the flag with the thirteen stripes, and British union, and finally in 1777 the American flag of the present design. The song "Yankee Doodle" is interesting. It originated in England about 1645 as a burlesque on Oliver Cromwell, and thus has served as a shibboleth in the two revolutions—the Puritan and the American. In its original English form it was "Nankey Doodle." The word "Yankey" was substituted for "Nankey" at the siege of Boston in 1775. The word "Yankey" originated as college slang at Yale in 1713. The spelling "Yankee" is of later date than the American Revolution. In addition to "Yankee" we have in this Revolution: "Britisher," "Tory," "Loyalist," "Red Coat," "Whig," "Patriot," "Liberty Boy," and others. The chief isolation devices were the innumerable revolutionary secret societies and other organizations.

The French Revolution was very rich in shibboleths: *Liberté, Egalité, Fraternité, Royaliste, Aristocrate, Monarchiste, Republicain, Sans-culotte*, the red cockade and the white cockade, the *fleur-de-lis* and the tricolor, the "Marseillaise," the simple classic style of women's clothes, the ornate court style, and similar variations in men's apparel.

The enormous development of revolutionary clubs was again, as in the American Revolution, the chief isolation device.

In the Russian Revolution we have "czarist," "bolshevik," "capitalism," "communism," "bourgeoisie," "socialism," "proletariat," "soviet," and other word shibboleths. The red flag was the main physical shibboleth, and once more the main isolation device was the radical club or society (soviet) which blossomed everywhere. This enormous proliferation of radical societies is characteristic of the beginning of all modern revolutions from the American onward. The names of the chief leaders on each side generally make some of the best shibboleths. The names of radical leaders are a little better than those of conservative ones for provoking antagonistic enthusiasms of love and hate: Czar Nicholas II and the Czarina, Lenin and Trotsky, George III and George Washington, and so on for any revolution.

By means of the shibboleths and isolation devices it at once becomes clear to everyone that the revolutionary society is split into two main factions. These factions fight each other during the revolution, and commonly continue under the same or different names as the political parties of the subsequent era. Thus the Liberals and Conservatives of present-day English politics go back through the Whigs and the Tories (which words are shibboleths of the Revolution of 1688) to the Cavalier and Roundheads of the Puritan Revolution.

The two main parties thus disclosed at the outbreak of revolution are the moderate reformers and the radicals. The moderate reformers want change but careful, slow, and legal change, and no change of a really fundamental nature. The radicals want fundamental change, which involves revolution, though as yet they do not comprehend this. At the outbreak of revolution the moderate reformers are always a much more numerous and respectable group than the radicals. It is always the moderates who organize the new "illegal" government which does emergency police duty when the decrepit old government shows itself without strength for the task. At an early stage in every revolution the moderate reformers become the regular "legal" government either by abolishing the old "legal" one or by gaining control of it and remodeling it according to their ideas.

Thus about ten days after the outbreak of the Russian Revolution czardom was abolished and the Duma was in control of the machinery of government. The great majority of the members of the Duma were moderate reformers, and they appointed a cabinet from their own number with Prince Lvov as premier. The members of this cabinet were liberal-minded and progressive men but by no means radical. Only one socialist was included, Kerensky, and he was a very mild one. This cabinet desired a moderate degree of reform along the lines of typical Western liberalism, as seen in France or the United States. Many of them were rich, and thoroughly representative of the propertied interests.

The French National Assembly which took over the government from the Bourbon monarchy was simply the old States General united in one body. It aimed to give France a strong, constitutional monarchy with the actual administration of affairs in the hands of the middle class. It abolished most of the old abuses, and did many things to modernize and improve the machinery of government. But it was thoroughly moderate in its measures. It had no desire to destroy the monarchy or even to limit its powers more than was necessary to safeguard these moderate reforms and to prevent a return to the old régime.

Similarly, the first American Continental Congress, that of 1774, was—to use the words of John Adams—"a collection of the greatest men upon this continent in point of abilities, virtues, and fortunes." These men desired an honorable reconciliation with the British government, and did nothing to prevent such a reconciliation but all they could to promote one. They desired constitutional liberty within the British Empire; such liberty as Canada or Australia now enjoys. They would have been perfectly satisfied with that. They were firmly resolved to resist anything dangerous to their own freedom, wealth, and power. But they were moderate reformers, not revolutionists. They had no desire to break up the British Empire or to found an independent nation.

The Parliament which in 1642 made war upon King Charles I was composed almost entirely of moderate reformers. It wanted a constitutional monarchy and was as much afraid of defeating the King too thoroughly as of being too thoroughly defeated by him. It wished the war to be a stalemate, or at most it wished its armies to win a very moderate victory—just enough to force a compromise which would reunite the monarchy and the Parliament in a permanent peace. It had no thought of overthrowing the ancient political and social institutions of England. Its leading men were wealthy landowners averse, both by disposition and training, to revolution.

At the beginning of the Protestant Reformation neither Luther nor anyone else had any idea of bringing on a revolution which would break up the ancient unity of Western

Christendom. The Protestants wished only for the reform of abuses. They desired to call a general council of the church in order to purify and strengthen it. Even after the bull of excommunication and the condemnation by the Diet of Worms, the command of affairs was in the hands of moderate and liberal-minded men. Albert, Archbishop of Mainz, the Archbishop of Trier, the Elector of Brandenburg, Duke George of Saxony, and other great princes, the rulers of Germany, held conferences with Luther and strove earnestly to bring about a compromise which would prevent any further outbreak and restore peace to the church and the Empire. They recognized the need of reform and were earnestly in favor of it, but they detested the very thought of revolution.

The early Christians had their millennial hope and expected that both the Roman Empire and the pagan religion would be miraculously destroyed at the second coming of Christ. But they had no idea at first, or for a long time, of overturning the political and religious order of the world by their own actions. They were obedient to the civil authorities in the face of the fiercest persecutions, and it was literally centuries before the thought of building a great ecclesiastical empire upon the ruins of the ancient civilization came into anyone's mind. The very popes themselves did not dream of it.

A revolution passes through its first phase with the moderate reformers in control of affairs. In this phase much good and necessary reform work is accomplished, but there is nothing which can be described as really revolutionary. Ancient and manifest abuses are abolished by general consent. The machinery of government is overhauled and repaired. The reform wave spreads from the great cities to the smaller towns and the rural regions. There is an "era of optimism." It seems for a short time as if everything is coming out all right, as if no further trouble need be feared. But the era of optimism is short lived, and the prospect of peace proves illusory. The reason for the breakdown of peaceable reform and for the failure of the moderate reformers is the persecution and emigration of the conservatives. This phenomenon has seldom received the attention its importance deserves. It is the main cause of the violence which succeeds the era of optimism. It brings on war, the triumph of the radicals, and the reign of terror, and is responsible for many of the subsequent developments of a revolution.

The shibboleths and isolation devices which come into use at the outbreak of revolution show a division of society into two factions: Christians and pagans, Protestants and Catholics, Puritans and Cavaliers, or whatever other names they bear. But a closer analysis will show that there are in reality three main factions, with many subfactions. These three main factions are the conservatives, the moderate reformers, and the radicals.

The conservatives, the "standpatters," are a minority group. So are the radicals, the true revolutionists. The moderate reformers are the intermediate and largest group. At the outbreak of a revolution and during its first phase the radicals combine with the moderate reformers because they are much too weak to accomplish anything by themselves. But this combination of moderate reformers and radicals quite outnumbers the conservatives. It persecutes them mercilessly, and from the beginning of revolution onward the conservatives seek safety in flight. The era of optimism is due to the fact that the conservatives have been largely eliminated while the radicals have not yet broken with the moderate reformers. The real revolution, when it comes, is not a fight between the conservatives and the combined moderate reformers and radicals. It is a fight between the moderate reformers and the radicals, after the emigration of the conservatives, who then function only by means of foreign armies and futile internal plots. The radicals win because the counterbalancing power of the conservatives has been destroyed, so far as the internal situation in the revolutionary society is concerned. Every conservative that emigrates adds just that much to the power of the radicals by reducing the really whole-hearted opposition to them. The great mistake which the moderate reformers make is in aiding and abetting, or at least acquiescing in, this persecution and emigration of the conservatives. The power which the moderate reformers gain at the outbreak of a revolution is due to the fact that they hold the balance of power between the conservatives and the radicals. With the elimination of the conservatives the natural equilibrium of the society is destroyed. The moderate reformers cannot any longer control events by inclining from one extreme to the other. But the mistake of the moderate reformers is very natural. They have suffered persecution at the hands of the conservatives. They have been taught by years of agitation to regard the conservatives as their natural enemies. The removal of the conservative opposition apparently facilitates reform and adds to the power of the moderate reformers. It actually does so just at first—until the radicals get well organized. The conservatives on their side do not attempt to come to terms with the moderate reformers. They are embittered by persecution which is a new experience for them, at least in the rôle of victims. They, first of any party in a revolution, realize that the issue can only be decided by force, and their flight is only a preliminary step to war.

The first mob outbreaks in a revolution are made by the combined moderate reformers and radicals enraged by oppression, but revolutionary war is almost always precipitated by refugee conservatives, enraged by the counter oppression of the moderate reformers and radicals. By deserting their posts these refugee conservatives really throw the victory to the radicals. They realize this themselves but they care little about it. They trust to foreign military power to crush both the moderate reformers and the radicals and to reinstate the old régime. The inherent despotism of revolutionary governments is revealed best in the treatment the conservatives receive during the rule of the moderate reformers. They are subjected to every form of indignity. They are mobbed. Their houses and goods are destroyed. They are deprived of all positions of honor, influence, or profit. They are denied freedom of speech and of the press. They are tortured and imprisoned. Sometimes they are killed. They live in constant fear. They are the minority, and flight is the only means they have of escaping from the intolerable tyranny under which they suffer. This merciless despotism of the triumphant majority is the cause of many subsequent evils. It arouses the passionate hatred of the persecuted conservatives. Once they have escaped from it, they do not rest until they get external military force to revenge them. But this appeal to foreign military force is the fatal mistake the conservatives make. It is commonly useless and plays directly into the hands of the radicals, insuring the success of the revolution. If the conservatives could only make up their minds to "stick it out" in spite of persecution and remain in their own homes or at least in their own country, the whole subsequent development of the revolution would be different.

Despotism of any sort, whether by the czar or the American "sons of liberty," is exceedingly difficult to enforce over any long period. The longer it lasts the more enemies it makes. The blood of the martyrs is the seed of the church— of the conservative political church as well as the ecclesiastical one. The effort and energy necessary in order to tyrannize over even a relatively small minority is so great as to weaken any autocracy, and will ultimately cause the downfall even of a tyrannical majority. The despotic majority after a time begins to lose adherents and presently is forced to compromise and to stop or greatly modify its autocratic behavior. But the conservatives cannot be blamed for not seeing the matter in this light. The tyranny of the moderate reformers urged on by the radicals is so unbearable that the conservatives cannot stand up under it and flee at the first opportunity. Their flight brings in the "era of optimism" but it is the beginning of real and serious revolution.

The tyranny of the moderate reformers and radicals in the first phase of a revolution is commonly overlooked or justified because it is the tyranny of the majority, but in point of severity it much exceeds that of the old régime.

At the outbreak of the Protestant Revolution Catholics fled by thousands from England, Scotland, Sweden, North Germany, and other Protestant countries. They emigrated to France, Spain, Italy, and all parts of Catholic Europe. Those Catholics who remained at home were greatly weakened by this desertion of their more extreme coreligionists and suffered persecutions only inferior to those of the Inquisition. The atrophy of patriotism is a marked feature of revolutionary periods. A Christian Roman loved a Christian barbarian more than a pagan Roman, and shed few tears when in its later days the Empire was invaded by Christianized barbarians. In the wars of religion during the Reformation, French Protestants welcomed the invasion of France by German Protestants and French Catholics betrayed their country to the armies of Catholic Spain. The same thing was true in the other countries involved in the religious wars.

From the very outbreak of the Puritan Revolution the persecution of the Royalists in every part of England subject to parliamentary rule was exceedingly severe. Early in the struggle, before any actual warfare, the Royalist members of Parliament, both lords and commons, deserted their seats and fled from London, which city was devoted to the Puritan cause. This desertion greatly weakened the moderate reformers and precipitated many serious evils, but the Royalists can hardly be blamed for it. They were constantly being subjected to insult and abuse, and went in almost daily danger of their lives. As might be expected, both the Royalists and the Parliamentarians sought aid from Scotland, which at that time was a foreign country though it had the same king.

The persecution of the Tories, or Loyalists as they called themselves, in the American Revolution is naturally not emphasized in the schoolbooks. From the very beginning of the Revolution these unfortunate people were fined and imprisoned, their property was confiscated, they suffered double or triple taxation, they were disfranchised. They were rendered incapable of holding any office. They were denied the right to sue in the law courts. They could not act as guardian or trustee. They were prohibited from practicing any of the professions. They could not be teachers, doctors, lawyers, or clergymen. They were not even allowed to engage in commercial or industrial enterprise. They were disarmed and not permitted to have weapons even for self-defense. They were driven from one colony to another. They were banished from the country altogether, and death was the penalty of return. These were only some of the legal disabilities they suffered. In addition to these, they were tarred and feathered; their homes and furniture were destroyed by mobs. They were ridden on rails and ducked in puddles and mud holes. Inquisitional committees visited and questioned them at all hours of the day and night. They were spied upon. Their mail was opened at the post-office. They were forbidden to worship God according to the dictates of their conscience.[1]

These matters are dwelt upon because the government set up by the American patriots is honorably distinguished among revolutionary governments for moderation and humanity. Even the most humane revolutionary government is much more tyrannical than the most autocratic despotism of non-revolutionary periods. The Jews in Russia under the czardom rightly obtained the sympathy of the world. Their condition was easy and fortunate compared to that of the Tories in America under the Continental Congress. As might be expected, the Tories eagerly welcomed the invasion of America by the Hessians. The Whigs called in the French, and both parties sought the aid of red Indian savages against their white fellow-Americans.

Both the persecution and the emigration of the privileged orders in the early days of the French Revolution are well known. The king's two brothers were among the

[1] M. Tyler, *American Historical Review*, pp. 24 ff.

émigrés, and with the other conspicuous refugees formed a regular political body which intrigued continually beyond the frontiers in Germany and Italy against the Revolution. This departure of high-placed ecclesiastics and high-born aristocrats, while important in its consequences, was not so disastrous to France as the great exodus of humbler nobles and propertied people which went on at the same time. The loss of this large body of conservative, respectable, and educated citizens had political and social consequences of the most serious kind. Many of the excesses of the subsequent period might have been avoided had this conservative force remained in the country to restrain the extremists and to preserve the balance of parties. The usual lack of patriotism is to be observed. Thousands of the *émigrés* served in the foreign armies which attempted the invasion and conquest of their native land. The revolutionists also sought the aid of revolutionary Germans and Italians against their Royalist fellow-Frenchmen.

The emigration of the more conspicuous czarists characterized the outbreak of the Russian Revolution. The exodus of the high aristocrats—grand dukes, princes, counts, and certain great ecclesiastics—was again not so important as the departure of the great body of the landed gentry, the lesser nobles, who were often good agriculturalists and possessed the only land in Russia on which there was any considerable degree of productive efficiency. But even the loss of these men was not so harmful as that of the industrialists—the directors, business managers, technicians, engineers, and other administrators whose persecution by the ignorant workingmen and abandonment of Russia went on at an ever increasing rate. The loss of these men caused a most serious paralysis of industry and was responsible for much of the want and suffering of the later period. All of these three classes—great aristocrats, landed gentry, and industrialists—were anti-patriotic and joined themselves to the various foreign armies which attempted to invade and conquer Russia. The revolutionists, in turn, sought the aid of foreign revolutionists against their fellow-Russians.

SELECTED REFERENCES

AULARD, F. V. A. *The French Revolution; A Political History*, Vol. I, chap. ii. Translated from the French (3d ed.). New York, 1910.

FERRI, ENRICO. *Die revolutionäre methode.* Translated from the Italian by ROBERT MICHELS. Leipzig, 1908.

HENDERSON, ERNEST FLAGG. *Symbol and Satire in the French Revolution.* New York and London, 1912.

LAVISSE, ERNEST. *Histoire de France Contemporaine*, Tome I, chap. ii. Paris, 1920–22.

LE BON, GUSTAVE. *The Crowd: A Study of the Popular Mind.* London, 1897.

LOMONOSSOFF, GEORGE V. *Memoirs of the Russian Revolution*, chap. ii. New York, 1919.

MATHEWS, SHAILER. *The French Revolution*, chap. ix. New York, 1923.

PHILLIPS, WALTER A. *The Revolution in Ireland, 1906–1923.* London and New York, 1923.

ROSS, EDWARD A. *The Russian Bolshevik Revolution*, chap. iii. New York, 1921.

SABINE, LORENZO. *The American Loyalists, or Biographical Sketches of Adherents to the British Crown in the War of the Revolution.* Boston, 1847.

SMITH, PRESERVED. *The Age of the Reformation*, chap. vi. New York, 1920.

VAN TYNE, CLAUDE H. *The American Revolution, 1776–83.* chap. iii. New York and London, 1905.

———. *The Causes of the War of Independence* being the first volume of a history of the founding of the American Republic, chap. xvii. Boston and New York, 1922.

CHAPTER VII

THE RISE OF THE RADICALS

Revolutions are all very much alike in their preliminary symptoms and in their early stages of development. Up to the actual outbreak of violence and even for a short time after the seizure of power by the moderate reformers the progress of events is strikingly similar in all of them. But very soon after the moderate reformers obtain control of affairs, differences in the development of revolutions begin to appear. These developments no longer conform to one type. From the era of optimism onward any individual revolution shows more and more evidences of differentiating itself into one of three classes. These three classes are: the abortive revolution, the moderate revolution, and the radical revolution. The underlying reason for these three forms of revolution is plain enough. There are three main factions in a revolutionary society which has arrived at the era of optimism. These three factions are the conservatives, the moderate reformers, and the radicals. At the outbreak of revolution the moderate reformers obtain control of the society. But it is evident that three different developments are thenceforth possible. The moderate reformers may retain power, or they may be overthrown by the conservatives, or by the radicals.

The first case—that in which the moderate reformers retain power all through the revolution—is well illustrated in the recent German, Austrian, and Czecho-Slovakian revolutions. This type of revolution, though marred by occasional

sporadic acts of violence and cruelty, is essentially peaceable. Its main objectives commend themselves to the
great middle class of ordinary citizens. The leaders of the
moderate reformers are persons of natural ability and of
considerable previous experience in the conduct of public
affairs. They obtain their (limited) objective with the minimum of loss and damage to the society they control. Such
revolutions are numerous in recent history.

The second possible development is that the moderate
reformers may be overthrown by the conservatives. This is
very frequently the case as the conservatives are generally
able to obtain the aid of foreign armies, e.g., the Hungarian
Revolution of 1848. Or the conservatives may win with the
help of foreign money and political influence but without the
need of foreign armies, e.g., the Russian Revolution of 1905.
But quite often the conservatives succeed simply by their
own strength and through the incapacity of their opponents
as Bismarck did in the Prussian Revolution of 1848. However it is obtained, the success of the conservatives in overthrowing the moderate reformers means the failure of the
revolution. The pre-revolutionary régime regains full power
and retains it for a period of indefinite length—varying from
a few years to a generation or more.

This rapid and effective reinstatement of the pre-revolutionary régime in an unchanged society must be sharply
differentiated from that reinstatement of a simulacrum of
the ancient régime which sometimes takes place at the end
of a successful radical revolution. The restoration of the
Hapsburg power in Hungary after the Revolution of 1848
was a real restoration. The same dynasty ruled with the
same power over the same society as before the Revolution.
The restoration of the Bourbons in France in 1815 was an

occurrence of quite another sort. Only a simulacrum of the old Bourbon monarchy was, or could be, set up. The restored dynasty had only the smallest modicum of its ancient power, and the society over which it ruled was utterly changed from the France of 1789.

Abortive revolutions, i.e., those which fail because of the inability of the moderate reformers to hold their own against the conservatives, are the most frequent of all revolutions. They are one of the most costly and wasteful forms of social action. There is much need for a thoroughly complete and thoroughly objective investigation of abortive revolutions. If the knowledge which would result from such an investigation could be popularized, a great amount of human suffering could be avoided.

Great as is the need for investigating abortive revolutions and moderate revolutions as well, the present study will be confined to the third form of revolution—the radical revolution. In this case the moderate reformers are overthrown, not by the conservatives, but by the radicals. This type of revolution is historically the most infrequent, but the phenomena which characterize it can be identified with comparative success. These phenomena are so clear and evident and so much alike that they can be classified with relative accuracy. The radical type of revolution offers the best chance of success to the investigator who attempts to reduce the phenomena of revolution to some semblance of scientific rationality. In addition to this the results of radical revolutions are of great and immediate social importance, and an understanding of them is to be especially desired. For the remainder of this study, therefore, attention will be more especially confined to the phenomena characteristic of radical revolutions. In radical revolutions the period be-

tween the era of optimism and the seizure of supreme power
by the radicals is a most obscure and confusing phase. It is
eminently a case of not being able to see the forest because
of the trees. The multiplicity of the events, the apparent
lack of rhyme or reason, logic or coherence in them, gives
the impression of a hopeless tangle. The length of this period
is indeterminate. It varies from a few months to several
years. Yet when the period is looked at as a whole, in relation to what precedes and follows it, the general trend of
affairs is plain enough.

The one thread through the maze is the rise of the
radicals. Whatever else happens, the masses of the people
are more and more influenced by radical ideas and the power of the radical leaders constantly increases. This is not
always evident on the face of things. There may be a number of "ups and downs" in the struggle, but the general
trend is toward radicalism. Amid all the confusing accounts
of crowds and tumults, of proclamations and declarations, of
accusations and counter-accusations, of civil war and foreign war, this trend must be kept in mind.

The social reactions of this phase of revolution have
been exhaustively studied by the Russian sociologist Sorokin, though not in so objective and detached a manner as
might be wished. Only the barest epitome is in place here.
New words and expressions come into the language to ex-
press new ideas and experiences. This is nothing peculiar
in itself. New words are always coming into any living language. But the number and variety of new words is much
greater in revolutionary times. It is an outward and visible
sign of a greatly increased mental activity. This increase in
mental activity is an excellent thing, despite the fact that
it is naturally somewhat confused and chaotic at first.

There is an apparent, perhaps an actual, change in standards of personal morality. There is an increased openness in speaking and writing about erotic and sentimental matters. There is probably, during this period, little actual increase in licentiousness as compared to the old régime. But it is indulged in by different people and in a cruder and more open manner than was characteristic of the exploiters under the former social system. There is a rapid change in the ideas regarding marriage, divorce, prostitution, illegitimacy, and similar social problems. The more intimate relations of life are subjected to some degree of rationalization and are freed from certain restrictive conventions and superstitions which have made them intolerable and hateful to great numbers of people. The net result of all this upheaval is beneficial. There is more honesty as there is more light. But the change goes on at so rapid a rate that necessary moral restraint is in many cases lost. Still it is easy to exaggerate the importance of revolutionary immorality. It is spectacular, but not of great moment. The vast majority of ordinary sex relations remain quite unchanged by any revolution. Such relations are essentially physiological and sentimental, and they are not subject to anything more than a very superficial change by influences of a political, social, or economic kind. Nearly all great revolutionary leaders are men of correct and even austere personal morals—in spite of popular superstition to the contrary.

During this period there is a change in industry which has important after-effects. The old system of ownership and control is breaking down. Men newly free, or still struggling to be free, from economic and political exploitation, naturally do not work so hard as during the previous period during which the inherited social order was—outwardly at least—still firmly established. They change from one job to another with great rapidity. They spend much time in arguments and debates, in listening to speeches, and in plain idleness. The routine of daily life is broken up. The immediate result is an increase in poverty, an acute shortage of food and of manufactured goods. But the more indirect and far-reaching results are of a most beneficial sort. The workingman's backbone is stiffened. He gains self-respect. He comes to a new realization of his importance in society. He demands and receives more consideration than formerly. He looks the world in the face. The old psychology of submission is broken down, and when sheer necessity finally forces him to go to work again, he does not have the old inferiority complex. This spiritual gain is no doubt worth the severe, temporary poverty which is the price paid for it.

There is also a change in the ideas regarding authority and subordination. The policeman, the magistrate, and the other rulers of the old society had been hated and feared, but obeyed. With the outbreak of revolution it becomes manifest that these authorities can be curbed and overthrown. Respect for any authority, except that of the revolution, diminishes and finally disappears. There is more autocratic government than existed previously, but it is exercised directly by the people concerned, who become their own policemen, magistrates, and rulers. It is an extremely crude but extremely vigorous authority, because it is an expression of the wishes of the people. It is majority despotism; that is to say, it is not felt to be a despotism except by the minority. The majority get a great relief of nervous tension by exercising tyranny over their former tyrants. Here again the immediate results are bad, but the ultimate results may be good. It comes to be generally recognized that no authority can claim any right except as it expresses the will, or at least has the acquiescence, of the majority. The rights of the minority should be safeguarded but they never are. In this respect revolutionary governments are not different from others, except in degree. All majority government is despotic—in its treatment of the minority. Nevertheless, the existence of some accepted authority, even though it be despotic, is a gain. It permits the new society to act consistently and with vigor. After a time the need for conciliating the minority is partially and incompletely learned—but learned it is, in some sort. Majorities are subject to change, and the majority of today may find itself the minority of tomorrow. So majorities at last learn caution, though they never learn real toleration.

The mobility of the population is a marked characteristic of this phase of a revolution. Enormous numbers of people are traveling, both for reasons of a compelling sort and from sheer love of moving around. The pressure of want; the hope of gain; the desire to participate, on one side or the other, in the stirring events that are taking place; the necessity of escaping from the country or of hiding until quieter times—all these and other causes effect great changes of population. People flock to the cities and scatter back again into the country. Towns fluctuate violently in size. A considerable section of the public becomes more or less nomadic. A fairly large amount of internal migration is found in any healthy and progressive society. But the amount of such migration in revolutionary societies exceeds that of any society in peaceable times. Yet, in spite of many evils which arise from it, the result on the whole is good. The cultural effect of seeing new places and coming into contact with new people is a gain. The necessity of making new adjustments is mentally stimulating. Old prejudices and archaic social inhibitions are broken down. The elemental wish for new experience meets with satisfaction. The whole *tempo* of life is quickened. Attention and interest are stimulated even when, as if often the case, the change of location involves great hardship and danger.

Changes of social status are as much in evidence as changes of location. Large numbers of people are suddenly hurled from the highest positions in society to the lowest. The places of these deposed ones are taken at this stage by those of a middle rank in the society. The places thus vacated in the middle rank are filled up from the lower class, and the empty places in the lower ranks are left vacant or partly filled by the deposed upper class. There is a social `avalanche. "That which was nothing has become everything." Nobles, generals, and high officials become menial servants, peddlers, and beggars. Aristocratic women become seamstresses, waitresses, and common harlots, while shop girls and workingmen's wives sit in the boxes at the grand opera. Ordinary lawyers, doctors, journalists, and students become persons of great power and high social position. Many representatives of the working classes—carpenters, stonemasons, farmers, and others—attain to positions of influence and importance never before open to them. This high degree of social mobility, in spite of its obvious drawbacks, is beneficial in its final result. There is a great increase of hope and ambition in the masses of the people. Everybody knows someone who has had a spectacular rise in the world, and everyone is trusting that his turn will come next. It is true that this new society is crude and vulgar. It is true that many of those who rise so rapidly do not possess the necessary qualities to enable them to retain their new positions, and they fall as rapidly as they rose. Nevertheless, this period of revolution is the great time of opportunity for the born leader of humble birth and small means. Journalists become secretaries of state. Private soldiers become generals. Small merchants become millionaires. The progress as a whole is too rapid to be stable, and a reverse process sets in; but the idea of equality of opportunity becomes popularized. This is one of the great and permanent gains of revolution. The notion of caste is at least partly broken up. The different classes are transfused. Equality of opportunity is never attained, but it is at any rate approximated. Political, social, or economic opportunity is always greater in any society after a successful revolution than before. But the opportunities, for the capable individual, are never so great in quiet as in revolutionary societies.

Mobility of mind in the general population becomes marked at this time. Governments, institutions, organizations, economic conditions, and all sorts of other things are changing so rapidly that the common man, in his own despite, is forced to become mentally agile in order to take care of himself in the general flux. He becomes more self-reliant and more highly individualized. His outlook on life changes often. He becomes skeptical about religion and many other things. He grows familiar with a great variety of ideas upon all sorts of important questions. His knowledge of the forces controlling society increases. He changes his allegiance to political parties rapidly and easily. He meets reverses resiliently. He adopts new points of view readily. He takes hold of a new situation with the speed which comes from practice. After the revolution he is twice as much a man as he was before.

It is the common opinion that crime of all kinds flourishes exceedingly in time of revolution. This opinion turns out to be badly founded. An examination of the data leads to the conclusion that no reliable generalization can be made upon this subject. Some revolutions (the French Revolutions of 1830 and 1848, for example) seem to be characterized by an actual diminution of ordinary antisocial conduct. It is easy to see how this comes about. The great body of criminals are enlisted, on one side or the other, in any revolution. Revolutionary activities and legalized warfare give an outlet to their energies. They are diverted from criminal practices. Of course they are still committing murder, arson, and robbery, but these actions, now having social consent, are removed from the category of crimes and are committed by all brave and patriotic men. The criminal becomes the hero. Other revolutions (such as the Puritan and the American) apparently have no ascertainable effect one way or the other upon ordinary crime. It is possible that very minute scrutiny might show some slight deviations, but certainly no greater ones than are usual in peaceable times. Still other revolutions show an increase of crime (the French Revolution of 1787 and the Russian Revolution of 1917). But the increase is not greater than is met with in non-revolutionary societies, such as mining camps and frontier towns, or perhaps such great cities as Chicago or New York. It would seem, on the whole, that ordinary crimes, as opposed to actions which have at least some color of social consent, are not affected in any predictable way by revolution.

The influence of revolution on the composition of the population is harmful. The number of the population is diminished by direct and indirect loss of life, though the absolute number of people in the revolutionary society may

not decrease. Quite generally there is an increase in the
marriage rate which in some measure offsets the loss of life.
The persons who lose their lives are generally, but by no
means always, the younger, more vigorous, and biologically
more fit members of the society. But in all these respects,
the effects of revolution do not differ from those of ordinary
war. Populations readjust themselves after a time. The
biologically fit increase, the unfit are eliminated, and normal
population composition is again reached.

From what has been said hitherto, it may be inferred
that all radical revolutions are of the same general type,
but this is by no means true. Even the most imperfect outline of the radical revolutionary process requires that some
distinction be made between religious and secular revolutions. In a very loose though real sense of the term, all
great revolutions may be said to have a "religious element"
in them. The social myth is essentially of a mystical and
religious nature. But admitting this to be true, there is still
a distinction between religious revolutions properly so
called (such as the conversion of the Roman Empire to
Christianity or the Protestant Reformation) and essentially
secular revolutions such as the great French Revolution or
the Russian Revolution. Religious revolutions are always
very much slower in their development. The conversion of
the Roman Empire begins in the time of Christ and continues to the final triumph under the successors of the
Emperor Julian—a period of more than three centuries and
a half. The Mohammedan Revolution from the Hegira to
the battle of Tours took one hundred and ten years. The
Protestant Reformation from the Wittenberg theses to
Richelieu's intervention in the Thirty Years' War lasted one
hundred and eleven years. Compared to this, the Puritan

Revolution from the meeting of the Long Parliament until the Restoration lasted twenty years. The American Revolution from the Boston Tea Party until the adoption of the federal Constitution lasted fourteen years. The Great French Revolution from the meeting of the States General to the end of the Directory lasted ten years. The Russian Revolution from the St. Petersburg general strike in March, 1917, until the inauguration of the new economic policy in the spring of 1921 lasted only four years.

In addition to their slower development, religious revolutions are much less complete in the changes they bring about. Perhaps half of the population of the Roman Empire were still pagans in the year 400 A.D. The Protestant Reformation cost the Roman church heavily, but even at the end of it there were more Romanists than Protestants in Western Europe. The reason for this is probably that religious revolution, as opposed to secular revolution, is incapable of demonstrating the truth of its contentions. The opposition is just as incapable of demonstrating their falsity. Equally intelligent and well-informed people can and do hold quite opposite beliefs regarding matters of a strictly religious nature. This always has been true and probably always will be. One person believes in praying for the dead; another person of equal piety and intelligence does not. There is no way of settling the matter. In the nature of the case, the belief cannot be subjected to experience for verification or disproof. The case is quite otherwise with secular matters which are subject to the test of experience. Nobody in England today believes in trying to restore the autocratic monarchy of Charles I, but there are plenty of Roman Catholics in England today anxious to restore the ancient papal authority. Nobody in America today dreams of restoring the United

States to their old status as British colonies, but there are plenty of agnostics and infidels in Rome today eager to destroy Christianity.

Religious revolutions perhaps show the same sequence of phenomena as secular radical revolutions but only in the most general way. The intensity and persistence of religious beliefs greatly exceeds that of secular ideas. No secular revolutionary fanaticism, however great, quite attains to the fervidness and continuity characteristic of purely religious fanaticism. As compared to secular revolutions, religious ones show great distortions. The sacrificial urge is enormously greater. Masses of people will do more and suffer more from purely religious motives than from any other motives whatever, except, perhaps, the elementary physical ones of sex and hunger. The social forces which operate directly and rapidly upon a secular revolution work slowly and imperfectly in the case of a religious revolution. In the present state of sociology it would be practically impossible to trace the revolutionary process in religious upheavals with anything like the accuracy possible in secular revolutions. What period constitutes the era of optimism in the conversion of the Roman Empire? It is impossible to say. Reasons might be given for three or four different periods. A few things are tolerably well defined. The development of the power of the bishops and councils is fairly clear. The growth of intolerance can be traced. The periods of persecution are known. The date of the attainment of formal legal status is familiar, as is that of the final triumph of the Christian extremists determined to stamp out all heresy as well as all paganism. Many things of this sort are recognizable. But the specific identification of the several stages of religious revolution is impossible at present.

It is the easiest thing imaginable to draw up an arbitrary series of stages and then twist and torture the data to fit this Procrustean bed. It has often been done—with different results in each case. But the process of investigating secular revolutions by the inductive method is different. A minutely detailed list of events according to their chronological sequence is drawn up for one revolution and the process repeated for other revolutions. These long lists of events are then compared and an ideal revolution plotted from the conformities of the real revolutions. When this laborious process is completed (and it is a very laborious process) the conformity of the secular revolutions to a type is immediately evident. It is not nearly so evident with the religious revolutions. That there is a revolutionary process common to both religious and secular revolutions is a matter of faith, not of knowledge. It is a hypothesis which seems to have a certain plausibility. But no attempt will be made here either to verify or refute it. It must remain a hypothesis. But that there is a revolutionary process common to all secular revolutions may be taken as certain. The percentage of coincidences is far more than can be explained by any theory of chance. Thus the Peace of Augsburg may or may not be the era of optimism in the Protestant Reformation, but the era of optimism in the Russian Revolution is as well defined as any period in history. It began March 15, 1917, and lasted about two months. So in the great French Revolution the abolition of feudal rights, August 4, 1789, marks a clearly evident era of optimism which began with the taking of the Bastile, July 14, and lasted three or four months. Similarly, in the American Revolution the era of optimism began with Washington's capture of Boston. Its high-water mark was reached when news of this event got round to all the colonies.

It lasted about three months—March to June, 1776. The era of optimism in the Puritan Revolution began with the execution of the Earl of Stafford, May 12, 1641, and continued until August or September of the same year, when the rise of the religious issue brought it to a close.

Nothing approaching a complete list of the events characteristic of revolutions between the era of optimism and the seizure of supreme power by the radicals is feasible in a short space. Still some additional ones should be touched upon and at least a few historical illustrations given.

A release of political prisoners takes place very soon after the assumption of power by the moderate reformers. Thus in the Puritan Revolution, Pym and many other political prisoners were released in August, 1641. The proceedings against Hampden, Prynne, and others were annulled and the courts of Star Chamber and High Commission abolished. In the American Revolution the militia prevented the royal judges from sitting, and persons under sentence or indictment for political offenses were released. The attempt of General Gage to seize Hancock and Adams was frustrated. A considerable number of political prisoners were sent to England to prevent their release by the colonial forces. In the French Revolution the political prisoners in the Bastile and other prisons were released, but the ordinary felons were left in confinement. In the Russian Revolution the political prisoners were released from their various prisons and the political exiles were recalled from Siberia and foreign countries on March 16, 1917, the day following the abdication of the Czar.

The surface co-operation of moderate reformers and radicals is illustrated in the Puritan Revolution by the various changes in the ministry when the Earl of Essex and the Earl of Warwick were admitted to the Council, Pym became chancellor of the exchequer, and later Falkland and Hyde were made ministers. The idea was that these men could work out a *modus vivendi* with the Parliament and such radicals as Hampden, Vane, and Cromwell. All these arrangements were short lived and only added to the general confusion. In the American Revolution moderate men like the majority of the members of the First Continental Congress tried to act in co-operation with such radicals as Samuel Adams, Patrick Henry, and Richard Henry Lee, but no common understanding could be reached. In all the various separate colonial congresses and conventions which met at the time, the same co-operation was attempted with the same lack of success. In the French Revolution the like futile attempt at coalition is illustrated in various stages by the recall of Neckar, Mirabeau's attempts at compromise, the efforts of the Girondins to save the life of the King, and the various attempts to mediate between the Girondins and the Mountain. In the Russian Revolution, on March 15, 1917, Kerensky, a socialist, was admitted into the government of moderate reformers headed by Prince Lvov. On May 9, 1917, this government was changed by dropping some of its more conservative members and adding five representatives of the soviet. In August, 1917, this government was again reorganized with Kerensky as premier. It lasted until November, 1917. All of these coalition governments were equally short lived, futile, and powerless.

One or more vain attempts to seize supreme power are made by the radicals before their final successful effort. In the Puritan Revolution, Charles I was abducted by the army on June 5, 1647, and on August 17 Cromwell and the army took possession of London and forced eleven of their most bitter enemies to withdraw from the House of Commons. Only the dangers threatening England from the Royalists in Scotland and Ireland saved the moderate reformers from overthrow at this time. In the American Revolution the radical leaders tried to gain control of the First Continental Congress without success. Various like efforts were made in the various separate colonial revolutionary governments. In the Second Continental Congress the radicals were defeated a number of times before their final victory. In the French Revolution the Mountain made a series of attacks upon the dominant Girondins from the summer of 1791 onward. The Paris Commune aided the Mountain by lavishing large sums of money on the poorest and most radical proletarians. Danton and Desmoulins were especially active in these radical efforts to stampede the Assembly. In the Russian Revolution there were radical and anarchist demonstrations and riots in St. Petersburg on July 16, 17, and 18, 1917. Nearly a hundred people were killed and several hundred wounded, but order was finally restored. The provisional government imprisoned some of the chief bolshevik leaders—Trotsky, Lunacharsky, Kamenev, and others—while Lenin and Zinoviev only escaped a like fate by the cleverness with which they hid themselves.

The government of the moderate reformers is subjected to attack, not only from the radicals, but also from the reactionaries and conservatives. In the Puritan Revolution this conservative attack forms a distinct period, the Second Civil War. It lasted from March to September, 1647. Royalist insurrections broke out nearly everywhere. A great Royalist army from Scotland invaded England. Cromwell defeated this army at the battle of Preston. Cromwell and Fairfax between them put down the English Royalists with great severity, but for a short time the danger to the parliamentary cause was considerable. In the very beginning of the American Revolution, various efforts were made by the Tories at armed insurrection against the revolutionary colonial governments. A body of sixteen hundred of them were defeated at Moore's Creek, North Carolina, February 27, 1776. They were very active in New York, New Jersey, South Carolina, and a number of other colonies, while all the time the regular British military forces, augmented by a great enlistment of Tories, were operating against the colonial militia. In the French Revolution, the King dismissed the Girondin ministry June 12, 1792, and formed a reactionary government. The Royalist revolt in the Vendée began in August, 1792, and there were minor Royalist uprisings in other parts of the country. While these conservative activities never came very close to success, they were a real bother and something of a danger.

In the Russian Revolution, the Moscow Conference of August 25–28, 1917, showed both the power and the wishes of the conservative and reactionary factions. General Kaledin, hetman of the Cossacks, supported by army officers, industrial leaders, and Duma members, demanded that the government take reactionary steps which would have undone the Revolution. Shortly afterward General Kornilov attempted a conservative coup d'état against the provisional government. His officers cheerfully announced that they intended to hang Kerensky. The attempt, as it turned out, was a complete and even a ludicrous failure; but for a few days it was a very real and serious danger to the Revolution.

The extreme incompetence of the moderate reformers in military affairs is one of the most outstanding features of the period of revolution during which they are in power. The army becomes demoralized as a result of this administrative incapacity. Defeat and disaster overtake it, and the revolution is brought to the very brink of destruction. This weakness in military management results from the nature of the government of the moderate reformers. It is government by a deliberative assembly acting through committees. This form of government is ideal for affairs of a purely political sort. The correction of abuses in local administration, which is the worst sort of tyranny, is admirably carried out. The reorganization of political divisions and subdivisions is successfully accomplished. The explication of the principles of government is set forth in documents of the highest order of merit. The political record which the moderate reformers make is always extremely creditable. Much of the political work done by the Long Parliament during the Puritan Revolution has become a permanent part of the English constitution. The Grand Remonstrance and the Petition of Right are political documents of the most valuable kind. The same is true of the Declaration of Rights put out by the First Continental Congress in the American Revolution and the Declaration on the Taking Up of Arms in the Second—to say nothing of the Declaration of Independence. The political work of the National Assembly in the French Revolution was of the same high order. The measures for the abolition of feudalism, the organization of the departments in place of the old provinces, the Declaration of the Rights of Man, and similar measures exhibit statesmanship of the best sort. In the Russian Revolution the work of the provisional government in such matters as the liberation of oppressed nationalities, religious freedom, and the organization of local political units was of the most excellent kind and constituted a permanent contribution to the welfare of the country. The advantage of a deliberative assembly for carrying out political measures of this sort arises from the fact that everybody "gets in on the deal." Compromises, "arrangements," and "understandings" allow all parties to exercise influence and all antagonisms to be smoothed out. The advantages of a parliament in these respects are so great that no other form of political government is at all comparable to it.

But military government operates on the exactly opposite plan. It is only efficient as it is absolutely autocratic. Blind, unreasoning obedience to arbitrary authority is the supreme military virtue. Legislative government of any kind means absolute ruin in an army. Nothing is clearer in history than that an army under the autocratic command of a very ordinary general is a vastly better fighting machine than the same army under the control of a deliberative committee. This is true when all the members of the committee, individually, are military geniuses, greatly superior to the solitary general. No principle of government is better established than that military affairs must be autocratically administered. Yet for some reason or other, ignorance, inexperience, or what not, the moderate reformers in time of revolution always try to govern the army by political instead of military methods. The results are uniformly and universally disastrous. The army is demoralized and defeated. The revolution is put in jeopardy. The government of the moderate reformers loses popularity and prestige, and the seizure of the supreme power by the radicals is greatly facilitated. In the Puritan Revolution the interference of parliamentary committees in military affairs resulted in the defeat and confusion of the parliamentary armies, and all but gave the victory to the Royalists. It is true that in the later stages of the struggle this was in some degree remedied, but the remedy did not come from the moderate reformers. It came from the pressure applied by the radicals, as a result of which the military power was more and more centralized in the hands of Cromwell. The incompetence of both the First and Second Continental Congresses in the administration of military affairs during the American Revolution is familiar to everyone who has read the history of that period. Even in times of the most extreme emergency such as that preceding the capture of New York by Howe—slowness in recruiting, lack of food, lack of clothing, lack of military stores, lack of money, hesitancy, divided councils—all the things which could make for failure and catastrophe were in daily evidence. Thanks to such conduct of affairs, the revolution came within an inch of being lost. In the French Revolution the wonderful victories of the revolutionary forces under the rule of the radicals have somewhat obscured the defeats and disgraces of the earlier period. The condition of the French army during the rule of the moderate reformers was almost incredibly bad. At the very time (April 20, 1792) that the moderates started war against Austria and Prussia the army was in the worst possible shape. The moderates at that time had been in power for three years.

The discipline was deplorable. The regular soldiers of the old régime had lost from six to nine thousand officers by emigration and mixed no better than water and oil with the revolutionary volunteers who had been drafted (to the number of over two hundred battalions) into the ranks of the army; moreover these volunteer battalions were for the most part ill provided, far below their establishment, some only existed on paper; none were trained as soldiers should be.[1]

[1] H. Belloc, *The French Revolution*, pp. 118 ff.

Four hundred thousand men should have held the frontier; such a number was in the estimate. But the government could count on no more than one-fifth that number. From the English Channel to the Swiss mountains only eighty thousand men were under arms. The Prussian army alone, apart from its allies, was three times the size of this disorganized and insufficient force. Panics at once ludicrous and tragic opened the campaign upon the French side. Had the armies of Austria and Prussia moved with rapidity at this moment, the Revolution would have been at an end.

The military mismanagement of the moderate reformers in the Russian Revolution was, if possible, still more insane. Nothing quite so suicidal as Army Order Number One (March 14, 1917) can be found in any other revolution. In all the history of army administration it is impossible to meet its match. It transferred the whole power of military command including the control of supplies from the officers to committees elected by the private soldiers. The appalling results of this order were immediately visible in the total ruin the of army. It is true that efforts were afterward made to correct this fatal mistake. It is true that in later months the Galician offensive succeeded brilliantly for a short time —only to end in disaster and shame. But it was too late. The demoralization, breakup, and final melting away of the enormous Russian army of four million men, all within the space of nine or ten months and during wartime, is one of the most amazing spectacles in history. In all the annals of wars and armies there is nothing to be compared to it. The soldiers simply quit and went home. The provisional government may not have been entirely responsible for all that happened, but it was in power and it had to take the blame. It is certain that it exhibited incompetence of a truly colossal sort in every military emergency. Even the attempted coup d'état of Kornilov, which directly threatened the lives as well as the political power of the cabinet members of the provisional government, was put down, not by them, but by the exertions of the St. Petersburg soviet.

After what has been said, it may seem like irony to call the phase of revolution during which the moderate reformers govern the "period of revolutionary peace." Yet such it is. With all its mobs and tumults, with all its internal insurrections and external wars, with all its kaleidoscopic social changes, it is an era of peace. It is the lull before the storm. Compared either with the period of revolutionary outbreak before it, or the period of radical rule after it, the period of the rule of the moderate reformers really is quiet, calm, and peaceable. All things are comparative, even revolutionary periods, and comparatively speaking this period is entitled to its designation as the period of revolutionary peace. In the Puritan Revolution it lasted from May 12, 1641, to December 6, 1648; in the American Revolution the dates are December 16, 1773, to July 4, 1776; in the French Revolution, July 15, 1789, to August 19, 1792; in the Russian Revolution, from March 12, 1917, to November 7, 1917.

The moderate reformers do much lasting good during their tenure of power. But a revolution is not the kind of social situation in which safety can be found in the councils of moderate men. A country in revolution is like a person suffering from a deadly cancer. The best surgeon is the one who cuts boldly. After months or years of moderate rule the condition of affairs in the revolutionary society becomes desperate. The government of moderate men ends in wreck. If the total ruin of the revolution is to be avoided a change must be made. The revolution must go onward, and go onward rapidly. Force and speed alone can save it. The concentration of all power in the hands of a despot is the only salvation. The time for moderation is past. The desire for a determined and able, even though ruthless, government develops enormously during the last helpless weeks of the rule of the moderate reformers. That kind of government can come only from the radicals. Their seizure of power is generally represented as the unscrupulous act of a desperate minority. Desperate it is and the act of a minority, but not unscrupulous, unless by scrupulous is meant an attitude like that of the pious Jewish soldiers who allowed Jerusalem to be captured rather than fight on the Sabbath. The radicals save the revolution precisely because they are the only people around who are not too scrupulous to fight on the Sabbath, when the enemy attacks on the Sabbath. In plain English, the revolution is on the point of being wiped out in blood and the radicals save it by wiping out its opponents in blood. This is exactly what needs to be done and what the moderate reformers are unwilling and unable to do. But the radicals, when they seize power, are a minority. They could not hold power for a week without the tacit consent of the revolutionary majority. The last and most important thing to be here noted about the period of the moderate reformers' government is the uncontrollable swing of the masses of the people toward radicalism. Radical leaders gain enormous influence during this interval. They become the most prominent and most trusted persons in the society. Their radical ideas excite popular enthusiasm; their slogans are repeated everywhere. Though the radicals are a minority, they have the genuine backing of public opinion. Without this they would not have the smallest chance of success. This does not mean that the public has become radical, but it does mean that the public is content to give the radical leaders a chance to show whether they can save the situation. The conservatives have proved their incompetence by long years of misgovernment. The moderate reformers have then been given their opportunity, and they too have been found lacking. Only the radicals are left, and at the very last minute the public allows them their chance. The motive which leads the public to allow the radicals to seize power is the hope that real leadership—the one desperate need of the society—may come from them.

The swing of the people toward radicalism and the rise of the radical leaders—it is all one process—is illustrated in the Puritan Revolution by the steady rise of Cromwell, Ireton, Blake, Monk, and the other radical leaders. When the moderate reformers were overthrown, December 6, 1648, the popular name given to the event, "Pride's Purge," shows how much the general public were disposed to rejoice at the downfall of the helpless parliamentary government. Irrespective of politics, everybody in England knew that the one hope of strong and able government for the country rested in Oliver Cromwell. It was this enormous prestige of Cromwell, both in the army and in the nation, even among those who did not agree with him, which really overthrew the Parliament.

In the American Revolution the Second Continental Congress, which met May 10, 1775, was subjected to continual pressure by the radicals to declare the colonies independent. The conservative members of the Congress were able to stave off such action for more than a year. But during that space of time there developed a great popular movement in favor of independence. The radical leaders, hitherto looked at askance, became very influential. They brought over to their side some of the most conspicuous and most trusted men in the country, such as Washington, Franklin, Jefferson, and Morris. Still it is a fact that the Declaration of Independence was minority action. If the question of independence had been submitted to a vote of the people on July 4, 1776, it would have been defeated. The majority of the citizens were not yet ready for such a decisive step. Even in the Congress itself "strong-arm" methods were necessary to get a majority for the Declaration. There is no doubt that some of those who voted for it did so only under pressure. Certain of its chief advocates were men of dubious records—"police-court cases" we should call them today. But the radicals, though they did not have the active support of the majority, did have a general sentiment in their favor which enabled them to succeed. Nearly everybody felt that the existing state of affairs was intolerable. The unsettled conditions of government greatly alarmed that large body of citizens who were not active partisans, but who did care about the security of their lives and property. The actual situation was a continual series of evasions. The colonies were pretending allegiance to the Crown while actually making war against it. The various assemblies, conventions, and congresses which governed the colonies were all technically illegal and worked at cross-purposes. The result was enormous confusion and injustice. Sober people dreaded a continuance of such a situation. It undermined the morals of the public. It destroyed the habit of order and respect for regular government. So, while it is true that the majority were not in favor of independence on July 4, 1776, they nevertheless felt a sense of relief that the radicals at last had been able to put it through—even by "rough-neck" measures. At any rate, the indecision, un-

certainty, and illegality were at an end. Something decisive
had at last been done. The decision, even if it did not meet
with their full approval, was felt to be better than the condition of hesitancy, evasion, and lawlessness which had
existed hitherto. So the Declaration was accepted as a *fait
accomplé*, and presently there was an undoubted majority
in its favor.

In the French Revolution the intervention of the Commune of Paris, which was much more radical than the Legislative Assembly or the National Convention, complicates
the question as to when the moderate reformers were overthrown. The Paris Commune mobbed both of the national
legislatures a number of times. At such moments of mob
intervention the radicals were supreme, but the moderate
reformers resumed control after the mob dispersed. So,
while the swing of the country as a whole toward radical
policies can be traced easily enough, there is no one date
on which it can be said that the radicals gained supreme
power. The fact is that they advanced to supremacy gradually and by a series of successive victories. On August 10,
1792, the Paris mob invaded the Tuileries and forced the
suspension and imprisonment of the King. This uprising
added greatly to the power of Danton, Herbert, Marat, and
Robespierre. Yet for months thereafter the Girondins normally controlled the government. The massacre of September added to the power of the radicals, as did their victory in
passing the law for the execution of the King, January 15,
1793. The defeat of Neerwinden, March 18, 1793, and the
treason of Dumouriez following it caused a violent reaction
against the moderate reformers. The Committee of Public
Safety was instituted March 25, 1793, and finally on June
2, 1793, the Paris Commune forced the Convention to sus-

pend and arrest the twenty-nine leading Girondins. From that date until the end of the terror there can be no doubt of the fact that the extreme radicals held supreme power.

If there is a question as to when the radicals gained supreme power in the French Revolution, there is no doubt about that matter in the case of the Russian Revolution. The date was November 7, 1917. Like all the other seizures of power by the radicals, it has come in for criticism on the score of being minority action. Like all the other cases, there is no doubt that it was minority action. Yet the effective weight of public opinion was with the minority. The gist of this matter was well put by President Lowell years before the Russian Revolution:

> There is a common impression that public opinion depends upon and is measured by the mere number of persons to be found on each side of a question; but this is far from accurate. If 49 per cent of a community feel very strongly on one side and 51 per cent are lukewarmly on the other, the former opinion has the greater public force behind it and is certain to prevail ultimately, if it does not at once. One man who holds his belief tenaciously counts for as much as several men who hold theirs weakly, because he is more aggressive and thereby compels and overawes others into apparent agreement with him, or at least into silence and inaction.[1]

If these words had been written expressly to explain the success of the coup d'état of November 7, 1917, they could not have stated the facts more accurately. The soviet really had a better case than is commonly believed. For months before its end the provisional government had been steadily losing popularity and power. The radical leaders, more particularly Lenin and Trotsky, had been just as steadily gaining in influence and prestige. Even before November 7 the actual power, as apart from the formal power, was already

[1] A. L. Lowell, *Public Opinion and Popular Government*, pp. 3–14.

in the hands of the soviet. The coup d'état was nothing but the announcement to the world of a situation that existed before it took place. The vast majority of the Russian people, the peasants, were not communists, but they trusted Lenin. They believed that he would give them possession of the land, and they had confidence in his ability to secure them in possession against all the efforts of the landlords to get the land back again. That was all they really cared about. They were not concerned with the struggle for political power except as it affected their land. They believed implicitly in Lenin's reliability upon this capital question. So they were quite content to see him overthrow both the provisional government on November 7, 1917, and subsequently the Constituent Assembly on January 18, 1918. A very small, but very vocal, minority of city people protested loudly at these proceedings, but the overwhelming mass of the population, the country dwellers, were acquiescent. They received their land and were content.

SELECTED REFERENCES

BELLOC, HILAIRE. *The French Revolution.* New York, 1911.

CAMBRIDGE. *Modern History,* Vol. VIII, chap. vi. New York and London, 1902–12.

GARDINER, SAMUEL R. *History of the Great Civil War, 1642–1649,* Vol. III. London, New York, and Bombay, 1893.

LIEBERT, ARTHUR. *Vom Geist der Revolutionen.* Berlin, 1919.

LOWELL, A. LAWRENCE. *Public Opinion and Popular Government.* New York, 1913.

ROSS, EDWARD A. *The Russian Bolshevik Revolution,* chaps. ix and xii ff. New York, 1921.

SOROKIN, PITIRIM A. *The Sociology of Revolution.* Philadelphia and London, 1925.

TREVELYAN, SIR GEORGE OTTO. *The American Revolution,* Vol. II. New York, 1907.

CHAPTER VIII

THE REIGN OF TERROR

When the radicals obtain supreme power they have three main difficulties to face. These difficulties are foreign invasion, domestic insurrection, and their own inexperience in government. They have, however, certain great advantages. In the first place, they are a select group. They are the ones who have proved fittest in a very ferocious struggle for existence. They are the victors in the civil war, the strongest men that the revolutionary society possesses. They are likely to be bolder, abler, and more determined than any rulers that the country has had within living memory. They are willing to act. As excitement increases, the demand for action is intensified. The reformer fails because he is limited in the action that he takes or that he is able to imagine. The indecision and caution of the moderate reformers have brought the revolution to the point of failure. The decisiveness and enthusiasm of the new rulers snatch victory from the very jaws of defeat.

The essential characteristics of the radical rule are physical and mental courage, boldness, determination, an absolute faith in the righteousness of their cause and in their own ability to govern, despite lack of experience. This enthusiastic boldness does more than enable the radicals to gain supreme power at the crisis of the revolution. It enables them to obtain the success of the revolution, because their boldness kindles a like boldness in the public. There is a general tendency in a revolutionary public, as in a peaceable one, to give a new authority a chance to prove itself. When the new authority is composed of men of real ability and of bold enthusiasm, it is able to carry the general body of the public along with it and to accomplish things which, looked at in the calm detachment of a later day, seem almost incredible.

Thus in the Puritan Revolution, the substitution of Cromwell for Charles I, of Monk and Ireton for Massey and Vane, meant the rule of bolder, abler, more determined, and more enthusiastic leaders. However loyal an Englishman may be to his monarchy he cannot but feel a glow of patriotic pride when he contemplates the splendid position of power and influence which England attained a short time after the government fell into the hands of these radicals.

Similarly, when the Declaration of Independence put the legal government of the United States into the hands of Franklin, Washington, Jefferson, Adams, and other such leaders their superiority over Howe, Dunmore, and the other colonial governors, to say nothing of George III and Lord North, is the most striking thing about the change. There can be no doubt that the American patriots were the ablest body of statesmen then alive in the world, and with every allowance for other causes the success of the American Revolution is to be ascribed largely to their ability.

So in the French Revolution the opinions of historians differ regarding the characters of Marat, Danton, Mirabeau, Robespierre, and the other great revolutionists, but there is no question as to the fact that they were the ablest rulers France had had for many generations, and their enormous success in the face of almost insurmountable obstacles must always remain one of the most wonderful things in history.

The Russian Revolution is of recent date. Most of its

leaders are still alive. The passions and prejudices which always accompany any great revolution have not yet had time, in this case, to die away. Any judgment regarding the character and abilities of the leaders must therefore be tentative. Yet the great dictator who was the real leader and guide of that revolution is now dead. There is already visible among the more able and competent historians a tendency to give Lenin a very high place in history. He would appear to be certain of ranking among the greatest men Russia ever produced, and to be on a par of ability with Cromwell, Washington, and Robespierre, if not on a level with Julius Caesar himself. As to the abilities of Trotsky, Stalin, Dzerdzinsky, and the others, it is too early to speak, but taking the lowest estimate of their capacity to rule a revolutionary society, they must be allowed to be superior to Lvov, Miliukoff, and Kerensky, to say nothing of the men that formed the last cabinet of czardom.

The degree of popular support and enthusiasm given the radicals when they seize power is seldom as great as that previously given to the moderate reformers on their assumption of authority. But whereas the moderate reformers commonly fritter away their popularity by halfway measures, the radicals utilize their initial support and presently increase it. They are generally aided in this by the mistakes of their opponents. The first of these mistakes is the ferocious and unqualified violence with which the new radical government is denounced. This ill-considered invective arouses the resentment of that great body of the public whose patriotism is superior to their partisanship. In addition, the opponents of the radical government frequently bring about the invasion of the country by foreign armies.

The effect of this is immediate and striking. The enormous majority of ordinary citizens are not greatly concerned about the internal strife of the various factions for power. They are greatly concerned when they find their country in danger of being conquered by foreign armies. They at once rally to the support of their government, whatever it is, and are enthusiastically behind it in its efforts to defeat the foreigners. The radical government might perhaps be speedily overthrown if the struggle continued merely as internal, partisan strife. But the full strength of patriotic emotion is handed over to the radicals by their opponents' capital mistake in calling for foreign intervention. The radical rulers are thereby made secure, if only they can defeat the foreign invaders.

In the Puritan Revolution, no sooner had the Independents gained power and beheaded the King than a campaign of the most unmitigated abuse was started against them. The supporters of the Prince of Wales (afterward Charles II) started to raise armies of Irishmen and Scotsmen to invade England. The ordinary Englishman was not highly delighted with the Independents, but they were at least Englishmen, while he hated the Irish as Catholics and barbarians, and he regarded the Highlanders of Scotland as little better than freebooters. He anticipated only murder, robbery, rape, and arson if these invaders were successful, and so he backed the Independents to the full in defending England against them. If, instead of denouncing the Independents as murderers and calling in these foreign armies, the Royalists and Presbyterians had united in calling for a new, freely elected Parliament, their chances of success against the Independents would have been very much greater.

In the American Revolution, the British government blindly denounced all the most popular revolutionary leaders. They refused to acknowledge the authority of the Continental Congress, and they called in Hessians and Red Indians to fight the revolutionary armies. All of these things gave a popular support to the radical revolutionary government which it never could have gained by any effort of its own.

In the French Revolution the wild denunciation of the radicals by their opponents, the summoning of Prussian, Austrian, and Russian armies to invade France, and the absurd manifesto of the Duke of Brunswick threatening Paris with "total subversion if the royal family were molested" produced an effect diametrically opposite to that intended. The patriotism of the French was raised to a white heat, and the radicals gained more power than they had ever expected to possess.

It might have been thought that by the year 1917 some tincture of psychological knowledge would be found among those persons, czarists and moderates, who desired to overthrow the radicals in Russia. It was not so.[1] The surest proof of the incapacity of these factions is found in the fact that they were blind to all the lessons of history. They repeated the old mistakes, the unmeasured denunciation of the radicals, and the calling in of foreign armies. To quote Ross in regard to the misrepresentation and vilifying of the radical government: "We cannot anticipate to what heights mendacious propaganda may rise in the future, but so far the anti-Bolsheviks hold the world record for the quantity

[1] The questions might be raised: Why are the moderates always incompetent? And in what ways are they incompetent? As propagandists? But propaganda has a technique, and most of this is emotion. The nationalist defense of nationalism is no less a distortion of truth. The outcries of the people who are frightened and in terror is not lying because it misleads others as to the facts.

production and marketing of untruth."[2] The whole chapter in Ross entitled "The Poison Gas Attack" is worth reading in this connection, but the other side of the business is the one which it is important to notice here. That is the reaction of the ordinary Russian, who was not a violent partisan, to this unscrupulous lying about his government and his country. The anti-bolsheviks either had no competent psychologists in their number or they paid no attention to them. Otherwise they would have known that such unmitigated lies as those of the nationalization of women and the Chinese executioners in Moscow could not but arouse the hatred of all patriotic Russians against those who were guilty of spreading such abominable falsehoods about their country. Similarly, the sending of American, English, French, Japanese, and other foreign armies to invade Russia caused all Russians who placed their country above their party to rally to the bolshevik government in defense of their native land. It is not too much to say that in this case, as in others, the radicals were secured in power by the stupidity of their enemies. The opponents of the bolsheviks foolishly maligned the radical government at the very same time that they gave it the chance to defend the nation against foreign invasion. By so doing they solidified its power in the greatest degree possible. *Quos Deus vult perdere prius dementat.*

When the radicals attain supreme power they are at once made conscious of the fact that they must rely upon armed force for their success or even for their safety. Their opponents are so angry at being hurled from power that they not only resort to vituperation of the radicals but openly threaten the radical leaders with death, so soon as a

[2] E. A. Ross, *The Russian Soviet Republic*, p. 283.

change of fortune shall occur. These threats are always made and are always exceedingly foolish and dangerous. The supreme power being in the hands of the radicals, they are in a position to answer threats with deeds. For every radical leader whose death is threatened, the event shows that a conservative or moderate leader actually dies. The radical leaders are not only threatened with death, but the foreign armies which invade the country frequently put to death such radical leaders as they manage to capture. The radicals, being thus warned that no mercy will be shown them in case of defeat, naturally devote themselves immediately to the military defense of the nation and incidentally of themselves. Thanks to the blunders of their adversaries, there is a great wave of popular enthusiasm in their favor. Patriotism and the defense of the country become identified with loyalty and obedience to the radical government. The radical chiefs become the great popular patriots and heroes because they are the leaders in the national defense.

The fusion of national patriotism with the radical social myth is the most important spiritual cause of the success of the military campaign under the radical government. The tremendous power of patriotic loyalty reinforces the other great "religious" power of the social myth, and soldiers intoxicated with this heady, spiritual "mixed drink" are invincible against anything like equal numbers. The actual military equipment of the revolutionary armies is frequently, though not always, poor. But within fairly wide limits this is not a matter of the first importance. Their better morale makes up for their poorer equipment. In any case the radical government, aided by the popular enthusiasm, fits out its armies as well as is possible under the circumstances. It sometimes happens that the revolutionary forces manage to equip themselves very passably by using the military stores captured from their enemies. Where the radical rulers show the greatest superiority over their predecessors is not so much in the military equipment of the armies as in the technique for the political control of the armies. This technique, speaking broadly, embodies itself in two institutions. The first of these is the military committee of the Parliament; the second, the political commissioners with the armies. The military committee of the Parliament is intrusted with supreme authority over the army, and is not interfered with in the discharge of its duties. By this procedure, which is a marked change from that of the moderate reformers, the vacillation, hesitancy, slowness, and compromise characteristic of legislative government are eliminated from the conduct of the war, where they would be disastrous, while they are retained in political affairs proper, where they are advantageous. By the institution of political commissioners with the armies, two objects are attained. The higher military commanders, frequently untrustworthy, are subjected to observation and control, and the lesser officers and common soldiers are kept in a constant state of enthusiasm and loyalty to the government by speeches, pamphlets, celebrations, and all the other apparatus of propaganda which the political commissioners (who are expert professional politicians) know how to use with the utmost effect.

Of late years a large part of this revolutionary technique for military control has been taken over by ordinary governments engaged in ordinary international war. In the late war the Parliaments to a very unusual extent abdicated their ordinary control of military affairs, while it was found necessary to employ a very elaborate apparatus of propaganda in order to maintain the morale of the common soldiers. It would seem that with the development of popular education and the general advance in civilization it is now somewhat more difficult than formerly to arouse the anger and hatred of the ordinary citizen to the point where he is willing to participate in mass murder. The change is not great, yet a somewhat larger volume of noise and exaggeration is requisite to arouse and maintain the war spirit today than to incite to mob violence and direct action in politics.

In the Puritan Revolution the Independents (radicals) when they overthrew the Presbyterians (moderate reformers) were already in possession of the best-equipped, best-disciplined, and most experienced army in the world. This was an exceptional piece of luck which radicals seldom enjoy. Nothing was needed except celerity of action which was attained by putting the whole military power in the hands of a committee of thirty-eight members of whom Cromwell was chief. This committee, under Cromwell's direction, gave orders to all generals and admirals and arranged all business, caucus fashion, before presenting it to Parliament. As there were only about fifty members left in Parliament after Pride's Purge, the committee was in absolute control. It merely registered its own decrees under parliamentary form. The rapidity of its actions may be judged from the fact that it had three armies in Ireland within three months of the time it decided to invade that country, and the serious part of its Irish War lasted only eight or nine months.

In the American Revolution, before the end of 1776, the radical revolutionists in the Continental Congress were able to pass the resolution which made Washington a military dictator in the full sense of the term. This resolution intrusted him with practically unlimited power, and while it was wise and necessary under the circumstances it never could have passed during the previous régime of the moderates. By its terms Washington had absolute power to raise, equip, and pay armies, to purchase supplies, to promote and demote officers, to levy upon the citizens for troops, to arrest malcontents, and in general to do what he pleased. Except for this centralization of power in one man during the crisis following the capture of New York by the British, it is difficult to see how the Revolution could have survived. The original grant of power was for six months, but it was subsequently renewed. After the expiration of the dictatorship, Congress appointed a committee of five members to visit the army, reform abuses, and provide for the welfare of the soldiers in co-operation with Washington. This committee was with the army for several months in 1778, and by its labors greatly improved the morale of the soldiers. During the course of the war various other committees of similar nature were appointed as occasion required. The Board of War of the Congress, the military committee of the Parliament, seems to have carried on the management of military affairs as well as could be expected. It had its limitations at all times, but it was much more efficient under the radical régime than it had been during the first phase of the Revolution. The tardiness of the Congress in supplying men and munitions for the army was due to its own weakness. This weakness, in turn, was due to the fact that the American Revolution was a very mild one. The misgovernment against which the colonists revolted, while real, was not serious. The Revolution therefore had no great wrongs to avenge and did not go to extremes. The hatred and bitterness of the factions, while great absolutely, were insignificant compared to many other revolutions. The leaders of the American Revolution were never in great and immediate peril of their lives. The war, as wars go, was carried on in a fairly humane and decent manner. Consequently, while all the leading characteristics of the revolutionary process are observable in this Revolution, most of them do not take on any striking or exaggerated form. Thus the Continental Congress never possessed the absolute power exercised by radical legislatures in more desperate revolutions. The commissioners and committees for army control exercised such authority as was necessary. But conditions were far less terrible than those confronting the French or Russian commissioners and committees, and their whole procedure was correspondingly more humane and ordinary. When a real crisis arose the dictatorship intrusted to Washington was practically absolute, but such crises were rare. The dictatorship though stern was not deliberately cruel, and the American Revolution was the most merciful and the mildest of all the great revolutions.

The French Revolution presents the strongest contrast to the American. In France the tyranny and viciousness of the monarchy and aristocracy had been long continued and extreme. The repression of the elementary wishes of the mass of the people had been excessive, and the ferocity of the Revolution was correspondingly great. When the radicals came to power the danger to the existence of France as well as to the lives of the radical leaders was very real and imminent. At the time of the organization of the first Committee of Public Safety, April 6, 1793, France was at war with England, Holland, Prussia, Austria, Spain, and Sardinia. Armies of all these nations were either actually on French soil or close at hand preparing to invade the country. At a great council held in Antwerp, April 9, 1793, the representatives of England, Holland, Prussia, and Austria agreed upon, and openly announced, the scheme for the dismemberment of France. The Prussians were to have Alsace and Lorraine; the Austrians, Artois; the English, Dunkirk. It was proposed to crush the Revolution by terror —"by exterminating practically the whole of the party directing the nation." In the face of such dangers France and its revolutionary leaders had perforce to conquer or perish. The Spaniards speedily captured Bayonne and Perpignan; the English, Toulon; the Austrians, Valenciennes. France in all its history had never been in such danger. The actions of the radicals in this extreme crisis were rapid, determined, and spectacular. The Convention intrusted the whole direction of military affairs to the Committee of Public Safety, a small group of nine (later eleven) men, led first by Danton and afterward by Robespierre. Carnot, "the organizer of victory," who was the best-qualified man on the Committee, was given practically sole control of army organization. The Committee backed up Carnot and the Convention backed up the Committee. There was practically perfect harmony and co-operation. It is the greatest and most successful example in history of how a legislature should conduct war.

On August 16, 1793, the Convention decreed the famous *levée en masse* of all Frenchmen between the ages of eighteen and forty. On August 23 the men between the ages of eighteen and twenty-five were called out for service at the front. The number of soldiers under arms was raised to 850,000. Carnot's system for provisioning and arming this great host was wonderfully efficient. All the best practical skill and all the latest scientific research were summoned to the aid of the government. "The Republic was an immense besieged town and France one vast camp." Political commissioners were sent to the armies at the front. They removed unsuccessful and traitorous generals from their commands and sent some of them to Paris to be guillotined. The majority of the older military officers, being aristocrats, had emigrated or had surrendered to the enemy. Lafayette surrendered to the Austrians. A new body of young revolutionary officers was organized. The path of promotion was opened to every private soldier who showed any military ability. Great numbers of such men passed through many grades of rank in a few months. Hoche, a man of the lowest birth, was a private in 1789. Four years later, at the age of twenty-five, he was a general of division and commander of an army of seventy thousand men. The extreme youth of the generals matched that of the political rulers. Robespierre was only thirty-three at the time of his execution; Danton was thirty-four. Marat was the oldest of them. He was just fifty when Charlotte Corday assassinated him. Napoleon was twenty-six when he was given the command of the army in Italy. With the supreme power in the hands of such young men, chosen only for ability, there resulted, both in the nation and in the army, a spirit of aggression hampered by no traditions and no routine. Contrariwise, the enemy countries were nearly all ruled by old, cautious, self-seeking, and tradition-bound statesmen, many of them in their sixties or seventies. Their armies were commanded by generals of like type. The enormous enthusiasm, energy, and vigor of the revolutionary government and armies were, in considerable part, due to their youthfulness. Their guiding principle was summed up in Danton's phrase: *l'audace et toujours l'audace.*

In the Russian Revolution, the military power of the nation was at the lowest point when the radicals seized power and the peril from foreign invaders was extreme. English, American, German, Japanese, and other foreign armies were in possession of various parts of Russia. Diplomatic negotiations for the partition of the country were being made by the enemy governments, and the speedy success of these arrangements, as well as the immediate overthrow and execution of the radical leaders, was confidently expected and proclaimed. The old army of the czar had gone out of existence, and the few troops that survived from the régime of Kerensky were totally inadequate for the defense of the country. The first need of the radical government was for a large and dependable army. The rulers of the soviet were men familiar with the history of the French Revolution, and they proved that they had not studied history in vain. The task of raising, equipping, organizing, and directing the "Red Army" was intrusted by the soviet to the Council of Commissars, and the Council of Commissars gave the job to Trotsky. By skilfully combining the appeals of communist idealism and national patriotism Trotsky in an astonishingly short time (about eighteen months) was able to put into the field a fairly well-disciplined and passably equipped army of more than five million men. The higher officers were, of necessity, mostly old czarist generals but they were under the watchful eyes of the political commissioners of the army, powerful officials (again copied from the French Revolution) who were responsible only to the soviet and its Council. The subaltern officers were young communists turned out in great numbers by the officers' training schools.

They had no great military knowledge, but were men adequate for their positions. The common soldiers, elaborately propagandized by the political commissioners, were much more enthusiastic and intelligent than the privates in the old czarist armies had ever been. The whole organization was inspired by great zeal, ardor, and courage. The chief radical leaders in the Russian Revolution were not young men like the French rulers. Lenin, at the time he became dictator, was forty-seven. He held the supreme power without intermission until his death at the age of fifty-four. Trotsky was forty-one when he was made war commissar. The other great soviet leaders were nearly all men of about the same age. Many of them were in their forties, some in their thirties, but only very few in their twenties. They averaged probably ten years older than the "giants" of the French Convention, and there was proportionately more deliberation, foresight, and sobriety in their conduct of public affairs. Their policies were very far from being either reckless or headlong. Their government was neither so highly spectacular nor so brilliantly successful as that of the "youngsters" of the Convention, but its permanent achievements were not less great.

The second great danger which confronts a radical revolutionary government immediately it attains power is internal insurrection. The public as a whole may prefer the radical rule to that of the conservatives or the moderate reformers. But both of these factions have a numerous and influential membership smarting under their defeat and humiliation and desperately bent upon regaining their former positions of wealth and power by any means whatsoever. They not only arrange to have foreign armies conquer their country, but also organize armed insurrection against the radical government, generally sinking their differences for this purpose. The radical rulers are thus obliged to give much time and energy to quelling these domestic enemies, and their efforts for the defense of the nation against its foreign foes are proportionately hindered.

In the Puritan Revolution the radicals gained little by cutting off the head of Charles I. Another Charles, his son, immediately appeared with Ireland and Scotland at his back and a large part of the English nation ready to make insurrection in his favor. The military genius of Cromwell and the extreme efficiency of his army prevented the insurrection of the English Royalists and Presbyterians from gaining any great headway. The uprising of the Royalists, under the Earl of Derby, was suppressed with little trouble, while the Presbyterian uprising never got beyond the stage of a plot. Yet for a time there was danger of a really great upheaval. The government maintained peace in England only by great exertions, and by retaining in the country large military forces needed for the Irish and Scottish wars.

In the American Revolution the necessity in suppressing the numerous Royalist insurrections and attempts at insurrection forced the Congress to hold numerous bodies of troops in various parts of the country when those troops were urgently needed to reinforce the armies engaged in fighting the British forces. The Royalist uprisings were all suppressed, but not until they had protracted the war, probably for years longer than it would otherwise have lasted.

In the French Revolution the insurrection in the Vendée was the most extensive and bloody of all the numerous wars in which the Convention engaged. Along with it came the revolts in Marseilles, Lyons, and Toulon. All of these revolts together required almost as great an expenditure of men and money as the foreign wars. In the Russian Revolution the domestic revolts were much more serious than they would otherwise have been because of the support they received from Russia's foreign enemies. Modern methods of communication made it possible for England, France, Japan, and other countries to equip and supply four great civil wars started by the czarist and moderate factions. These conflicts, headed by Kolchak, Dennikin, Yudenich, and Wrangel, all ended in the triumph of the soviet, but not until millions of men had lost their lives and billions of dollars' worth of property had been destroyed. These revolts, had they been purely internal, would have involved little loss or bloodshed.

The third great difficulty met with by the radical revolutionary leaders when they assume power is their own inexperience in government. This difficulty is not so serious as the foreign wars or the domestic revolts but it is sufficiently troublesome. What is commonly known as "the government" of a civilized country is merely a cabinet or council of chief executives numbering only a score or so of persons. The actual carrying out of any policies which these high officials may decide upon requires the co-operation of thousands and tens of thousands of subordinate officials of all sorts: generals, admirals, ambassadors, consuls, judges, prosecutors, and so forth all the way down to clerks and office boys. When the radicals attain supreme power they find that this huge organization of officials is made up of persons appointed by the previous moderate or conservative rulers and that it is naturally in sympathy with them. Many of these officials take the only proper attitude for government employees, which is that they are the servants of their country and that it is their duty to do their work to the best of their ability no matter into whose hands the government may fall. But a certain number of officials do not hold this view. Their partisanship is stronger than their patriotism. Some of them resign at this critical juncture, a procedure which, while reprehensible, is not treacherous. Some go on strike, but a large number sabotage the radical government. They continue to hold their positions and to draw their pay but they systematically obstruct the carrying out of the government's policies as much as they dare, and they betray it to both its foreign and its domestic enemies.

But this turns out to be a phenomenon occurring in all government and all institutions. It works against the success of radical change. It causes an enormous amount of confusion, delay, waste, and destruction, at first, but it is presently stopped by the application of a little firmness. The great body of civil servants are dull, unenergetic persons, dreadfully afraid of losing their jobs and their pensions, and inordinately attached to petty distinctions of official rank. All that is necessary to bring them into line is to discharge a few hundred of the worst offenders without benefit of pension, and to demote a few hundred others. If it becomes necessary to execute a small number of the officials in the higher grades whose activities have been especially intelligent and dangerous, the revolutionary party is without the ordinary inhibitions that prevent such drastic action in feebler and more conservative governments. The really serious part of the business is likely to be that the radicals cannot find enough qualified men in their own ranks to take the place of the old-time civil servants. The inexperience of the radical rulers accounts for many acts which give their subordinates just cause for complaint.

It is needless to weary the reader with detailed historical

illustrations of these "white collar" revolts. One example is as good as a dozen—they are all very much alike. When Trotsky became war commissar of the soviet, some two thousand officials of the War Department went on strike, hoping thus to prevent the organization of the Red Army. Trotsky gave the strikers three days' notice. After that time their positions would be filled from a list of applicants. Most of the strikers returned to work within the time set. Those who did not were discharged with the loss of all pension rights. Within a few days many of the men thus discharged were back begging for jobs. A few were taken back, but given lower positions and less pay than they had formerly received.

The effort of the radical government to raise and train an adequate army takes time. In the interval the foreign armies—if there are foreign armies—advance farther and farther into the country. They come within striking distance of the capital. The radical government may be forced to remove to some other city. The whole country is in a state of wild excitement. The internal insurrections and plots of insurrection still further increase the general alarm. The treachery and sabotage of the bureaucratic officials threaten additional disaster. The finances are in desperate shape. Public feeling is strained to the highest point of tension. Some avenue of release for all this accumulated nervousness must be provided. The avenue of release is the reign of terror.

A reign of terror is psychologically akin—in some of its aspects at least—to an old-fashioned Methodist revival meeting. Its primary function is to serve as a safety-valve for the discharge of wrought-up emotions. It is the phase of revolution which most strikes the popular imagination because of its dramatic qualities. This is natural, for the terror—so far as it is planned and executed with definite purpose—is deliberate melodrama acted in real life. Like the melodrama of the theater, however, the performance that goes on behind the scenes is quite different from the show as the audience sees it. The terror presents itself as a wild orgy of unrestrained passion. Actually, it may be an elaborately planned and carefully worked-out stage show for purposes of emotional catharsis, which, according to the best authorities on such matters, is the purpose of all stage tragedy. The terror is not so bloody as is often assumed. This, at least, is the contention of Kropotkin, who has studied the matter exhaustively. He maintains that the terror is the least bloody of all phases of a revolution, and that it is not a horrible series of atrocities perpetrated by a savage mob upon innocent and helpless victims. It is, he would have us believe, a merciful plan of action that results in the saving of a dozen or a hundred lives for every one that it costs. According to this view, it is not an unrestrained uprising of all the lowest, most vicious, and most criminal elements of society. It is a drama played by the shrewdest and most far-sighted men in the country for the purpose of saving the nation from destruction. Mobs are used and massacres, but they are only stage mechanisms, utilized to create an illusion before a world-audience.

This view of a terror appears strange to those not familiar with the subject. But a detailed study of the actual technique employed by radical revolutionary governments in any reign of terror seems to substantiate Kropotkin's hypothesis to a considerable degree. He says that a reign of terror is just what the name implies. It is a reign, not an anarchy. It is an organized, governmental régime set up with a calculated purpose of social control. Again it is a reign, not of death and destruction, but of terror or fear of death and destruction, which is a different thing. The essential result aimed at is terror. Death and destruction may be necessary to produce the terror, but they are purely incidental. They are of the nature of stage technique employed only in so far as is requisite for the required effect. A terror is a scheme for scaring people. He claims that its purpose is beneficent because it aims to deter people from starting a civil war. The most important mechanism of a terror is not the killing of people, but the threatening of them. There is set in motion a most elaborate propaganda for producing fear. The radical rulers employ the most terrible and menacing language in innumerable speeches. Their endless oratory abounds in the most fearsome pronouncements of the dreadful danger that everybody will incur who disobeys or revolts against the existing government. The impression is carefully created that everybody is being watched and that the least hostile move means instant death. The most sinister and frightful rumors of the omniscience and vengefulness of themselves are industriously circulated by the radical rulers through the agency of trusted subordinates. The scheme, in order to be successful, requires that all this alarmist eloquence be substantiated by a certain number of highly dramatic executions carried out in such a manner as to give the impression that they are enormously more numerous than is really the case. All the means for producing this effect are studied with as much care as Mr. Ziegfeld gives to his most elaborate theatrical productions.

It is a curious fact that even intelligent people, who take the extravagant rhetoric of professional politicians at the proper discount under ordinary circumstances, become credulous in times of excitement. Any terror would be a hopeless failure if it were not for popular credulity. The rulers of a terror depend for success upon the fact that rumors rapidly become exaggerated and that impossible things can be believed under emotional stress. According to Ross, great use is also made of the snobbishness which characterizes civilized societies. A terror is a great exploitation of snobbery. The execution of one aristocrat is enormously more effective than the execution of a hundred laborers. The terrorists put a few dukes and princes to death and fill a million tradesmen and mechanics with abject alarm for their lives. The psychology of snobbery requires a point of connection between the nobleman and the common man, so a certain number of clerks and farm hands are sent to the guillotine along with the marquises and the millionaires in order not to snub the plebeians and in order to convince them that they are in the same danger as the wealthy and powerful. But the number of proletarians killed is small, and they are mostly idlers and toughs. The country is at war, and the rulers do not wish to kill useful and industrious workingmen.

A few historical illustrations will help to show the mechanics of a terror. The massacres and reign of terror instituted in Ireland by Oliver Cromwell during the Puritan Revolution stand out clearly even in the bloodstained history of that country. To this day, "The curse of Cromwell be upon you" is the most fearsome imprecation which any Irishman can invoke. The statistical evidence shows beyond doubt that Cromwell's conquest of Ireland was the least bloody of any in all its long history. His whole procedure, as his letters to Parliament show, was a scheme to terrify the Irish people so that they would not dare to re-

sist him. His policy had the desired effect, and he conquered
the country with a minimum loss of life. At the very beginning of the war he ordered two massacres, which he carried
out in the most spectacular manner possible. He accompanied these massacres with the most dreadful threats
against all who should dare to oppose him. Those two massacres were all that took place. They were all that were
necessary. Cromwell took care that a goodly number of
enemy soldiers and citizens should escape in the midst of
the slaughter. These persons, as he expected, fled to all parts
of the island, spreading the most extravagant stories of the
number of people killed. Cromwell was not a ferocious and
bloody-minded lunatic. He was one of the most shrewd and
self-controlled men who ever lived. No man in history ever
more carefully calculated beforehand just what the effect of
his actions would be. Circumstances were such that it was
necessary for him to conquer Ireland and to reduce it to
such a condition of terror that it would not dare to rebel
again for some time. It was necessary for him also to save
his troops as much as possible for the war in Scotland, which
had already begun, and which was much more dangerous to
his power. Above all, it was necessary for him to act quickly.
The deliberate massacre of forty-two hundred men, two-
thirds of them English, was his solution of the problem.
By that action he subdued the island in less than nine
months. He lost only a few hundred of his own troops, and
three large Irish armies, then in the field, dissolved from
mere terror as soon as the Puritan army approached them.
If Cromwell had conducted his campaign according to the
usual methods he would have had to fight all three of the
Irish armies. There cannot be any doubt that he would have
been victorious, and there is equally little doubt that he

would have killed at least thirty thousand Irishmen and lost
probably ten thousand of his own troops, while the war
would have lasted two or three years. Cromwell claims in
his official reports that his policy resulted in a great saving
of life. Whatever may be thought of the atrocity of such a
policy, there can be no doubt that Cromwell's claim was
correct. His system of terror in England involved almost no
loss of life at all. He instituted a spy system of moderate
size. It cost three hundred thousand dollars a year, but he
succeeded in creating the illusion that it was a hundred
times greater than it actually was. His main reliance was
upon a series of carefully thought-out threats which prove
his capacity as a psychologist. One of these threats was that
he would have every member of the royal family assassinated if an attack was made upon him. The threat was an
absurd one. No members of the royal family were in England, and he could not get at them in the various royal
courts on the Continent, where they had taken refuge. But
Cromwell took great care that his enemies should not know
how absurd his threat was. On the contrary, they believed
it implicity, and no great armed revolt occurred in England
during the Protectorate. It is certain that Cromwell had
more numerous and more violent enemies than Charles I.
Yet he kept them in such fear that no civil war was raised
against his government. He was no Charles I. He spared
the lives of tens of thousands of Englishmen who might have
been killed if the Royalists and Presbyterians had not been
too frightened to start an armed revolt. Cromwell attained
this result by the execution of about twenty-five men and
the imprisonment (never the long imprisonment) of a few
hundred.

As might be expected, the terror in the American Revolution was a mild one. The Loyalists were numerous, comprising between a quarter and a third of the whole population. At certain crises of the war it was absolutely essential to terrorize them so that they would not rise in armed rebellion. Thus a number were executed at Kingston, New York, during the crisis caused by Burgoyne's invasion. That part of New York State was so denuded of revolutionary troops that a Loyalist uprising there must have resulted in the capture of Albany and the escape of Burgoyne. The terror was worst in the Carolinas. About a hundred Tories were put to death in the crisis after the battle of Cowpens in South Carolina, October 8, 1780. Ten of them were hanged from one large tulip tree which remained standing for many years after and was an object of great popular curiosity. But such episodes were not frequent. For the most part the terror was bloodless. The committees generally contented themselves with stripping the Loyalists naked, coating them well with tar and feathers, and exhibiting them around the town in that guise. Spying and fearful threats proved the most efficient means of terrorization. A list of nearly five hundred persons were proclaimed traitors in Pennsylvania but only two were actually executed. The terror though mild was very efficient. Only about twenty thousand Loyalists actually took up arms during the six years of war. The terror unquestionably prevented the revolt of several times that number.

The terror of the French Revolution is by far the most famous. But its fame far exceeds its real importance. One hundred and seventy-eight revolutionary tribunals were set up in various parts of the country. That of Paris guillotined 2,625 persons. The total number of victims in all France was about 17,000, including 1,200 women. Not all were aristocrats; 4,000 were peasants and 3,000 workingmen. These numbers in themselves are great and horrible, but they are quite insignificant compared to the number of lives lost either in the internal insurrections or the foreign wars. More than 400,000 persons perished in the revolt of the Vendée, while 700,000 French soldiers were killed in the foreign wars from 1792 to 1800. If it be calculated that the terror did no more than prevent one other revolt such as the Vendée, it saved twenty-five lives for every one it cost. There can probably be little doubt that it did more than that. It was horrible, atrocious, and devilish beyond words, but it was effective, as the behavior of the enemies of the Revolution proved. Even though the terror in the hands of the leaders of revolution is conceived merely as a form of civil warfare, a device for securing at the least expense the ends for which revolutions are inaugurated, it is always something more. It is like the revolution itself—a great natural phenomenon—a phenomenon which can be controlled, more or less, and directed, but not wholly and forever suppressed.

As might be expected of the French, the "Great Terror" was most effectively staged. The act called "The Destruction of Lyons" is a good example. This city, the second in size in France, revolted against the Convention. A great army was sent to conquer it. It was solemnly proclaimed that all the inhabitants of Lyons were to be put to death. The city was to be totally destroyed. No city was ever to be built on the site. The very name of Lyons was to be blotted out forever. Great care was taken to promulgate this news in all cities where revolt was likely. After the capture of the city, batches of people were taken out and shot—care being taken that a goodly number escaped to carry the information broadcast of the total extirpation of the inhabitants. The actual number of executions was 1,684, a loss of population so small as to be imperceptible in a place the size of Lyons. The "destruction" of the city was of a piece with the "extirpation" of its inhabitants. A large number of workingmen were hired who went through the motions of wrecking some buildings. They were political appointees perfectly aware of the fact that all that was expected of them was the appearance of activity. Large numbers of people from certain suspected cities were given a glimpse of the "destruction." While they were looking a certain number of buildings actually had to be torn down to create the illusion of reality. These visitors were informed, which was true, that 400,000 francs a day was being paid to the wreckers. The visitors were then expedited to their own cities. The actual destruction was small, but this fantastic melodrama produced the desired effect. During the most critical months of the Revolution, October, 1793, to January, 1794, it was commonly believed all over France as well as abroad that Lyons had been totally destroyed and its inhabitants slaughtered. A dozen other French cities seething with revolt became quiet in an instant, and a critical danger to the Revolution was removed.

Little needs to be said about the "Red Terror" of the Russian Revolution. It was precipitated by the attempted assassination of Lenin, August 30, 1918. It lasted into 1919. The circumstances were parallel to those of the French Terror. The nation was encircled by foreign invaders and numberless counter-revolutionary conspiracies were on foot within the country. The total number killed is not known exactly. According to the report of the Tcheka (the revolutionary tribunal), 6,185 persons were put to death by its orders in 1918 and 3,456 in 1919. The reports of the local and district Tchekas are not available. At any rate, the terror accomplished its purpose, the internal enemies of the Revolution ceased to plot, and the hard-pressed Russian armies had a chance to beat off their foreign enemies. The Russian Terror was much less ferocious, and much less dramatic, than the French. No guillotine was set up in the Red Square in Moscow. There was no audience of women who sat knitting during the executions and brought their children to see people guillotined as calmly as they took them to see a puppet show. Dzerdzinsky was much inferior as a stage manager to Fouquier-Tinville. There was only one effective mass execution, that of five hundred counter-revolutionists, in Petrograd, in September, 1918. But this one was well handled. Soon all the newspapers were reporting that thousands of people were being shot in Petrograd and Moscow every day. According to these widely extravagant reports, the whole population of the two cities must have been killed several times over. The terrorists knew, of course, that the newspapers would do this. They co-operated with the Tcheka in creating this terror. The soviet gained the reputation of being a hundred or a thousand times as bloody as it really was. But all these rumors helped to scare the enemies of the Revolution. They are the tactics of revolution; just as defamation of your enemy is part of the tactics of war.

The rulers of a terror make use of fanatics and of a certain amount of mob violence. In consequence, there is frequently a destruction of valuable art objects associated with the old régime. Much priceless stained glass in the English cathedrals was broken by the Puritans. The royal statues and other regal insignia destroyed by mobs in the American

Revolution were of small artistic value, but this was pure good fortune. The destruction of the French royal tombs at St. Denis was a great artistic loss, hardly compensated for by the psychological advantage gained. The Russian Revolution is perhaps an honorable exception. Even in the midst of the terror, the soviet carefully guarded the great artistic treasures of Russia.

The terror furnishes a necessary avenue of release to the overwrought nerves of people in extreme danger. It is at the same time the revenge of a social class for what it regards as a social injustice long endured submissively and in silence. It is the eruption of the volcano.

SELECTED REFERENCES

Cambridge Modern History, Vol. VIII, chap. ix. New York and London, 1902–12.

GWYNN, STEPHEN L. *The History of Ireland*, chap. xxviii. London, 1923.

HAZEN, CHARLES DOWNER. *The French Revolution and Napoleon*. chap. v. New York, 1917.

JÁSZI OSZKAR. *Revolution and Counter-Revolution in Hungary*. London, 1924.

KAUTSKY, KARL. *The Dictatorship of the Proletariat*. London, 1919.

———. *Terrorism and Communism: A Contribution to the Natural History of Revolution*. London, 1920.

———. *Von der Demokratie zur Staats-Sklaverei; eine Auseinandersetzung mit Trotzki*. Berlin, 1921.

KROPOTKIN, PETER A. *The Great French Revolution, 1789–1793*, chaps. xvi ff. Translated from the French by N. F. DRYHURST. New York, 1900.

LE BON, GUSTAVE. *The Psychology of Revolution*. London, 1913.

LECKY, WILLIAM E. H. *The American Revolution, 1763–1783*, chap. iii. New York, 1906.

LENIN, NIKOLAI (ULIANOV, V. I.). *The Proletarian Revolution and Kautsky the Renegade*. New York, 1920.

LENIN, NIKOLAI (ULIANOV, V. I.). *The State and Revolution: Marxist Teaching on the State and the Task of the Proletariat in the Revolution.* London, 1919.

MARX, KARL, *Revolution and Counter-Revolution; or Germany in 1848.* London and New York, 1896.

ROSS, EDWARD A. *The Russian Soviet Republic.* New York and London, 1923.

SPARGO, JOHN. *The Psychology of Bolshevism.* New York and London, 1919.

SZENDE, PAUL. "Soziologie der Gegenrevolution," *Jahrbuch für Soziologie,* II, 1926.

TROTSKY, LEON (BRONSITEIN, LEO D.) *The Defence of Terrorism (Terrorism and Communism): a Reply to Karl Kautsky.* (Also known as *Dictatorship vs. Democracy*). London, 1921.

VAN TYNE, CLAUDE H. *The American Revolution, 1776–1783,* chap. x. New York and London, 1905.

CHAPTER IX

THE RETURN TO NORMALITY

A revolution dies out in a curiously insignificant and almost inconsequential way. Popular interest, and even historical interest, largely ceases with the end of the terror. If the revolution has succeeded, what happens afterward does not matter. What happens afterward is so commonplace and undramatic, compared with what has preceded, that it is incapable of gaining or holding any considerable degree of public interest. A revolutionary terror cannot originate except in a society where popular feeling is wrought up to the highest degree of intensity. It can continue only so long as this frantic orgy of emotion lasts. But as before stated, emotional energy is like physical energy in that there is only so much of it. After a few months it becomes exhausted and a condition of lethargy ensues. A period of emotional fatigue follows the period of emotional excess. This is the reason why the last end of a revolution is so uninteresting.

The aftermath of a political orgy is a period of economic chaos. The enormous war expenses, the uncertainty as to the government's future, the general paralysis of trade and commerce, the inexperience of many officials in charge of the public finances—all these and various other conditions combine to produce an economic situation of the most dangerous sort. It is usually impossible for the revolutionary government to raise by taxation, or to borrow, more than a very small fraction of the money imperatively needed. So recourse is had to two other instrumentalities: confiscation

186

and the printing press. During, or shortly after, the political terror, the property of the conservatives, and sometimes that of the moderate reformers, is likely to be confiscated. The Rump Parliament confiscated the estates of those who rebelled against its authority, and Cromwell laid a 10 per cent capital levy upon the property of all Royalists. The property of the Tories was confiscated to the amount of over $35,000,000 during the American Revolution—a sum which, considering the poverty of those times, was really enormous. Robespierre confiscated the estates of the aristocrats and divided them among the three million French peasants whose descendants own them to this day. Both the landed estates of the czarist nobles and the factories and other property of the Russian bourgeoisie were confiscated by the soviet. But considerable as is the amount of money realized by this means, it is quite inadequate to meet the costs of the national defense. So the printing press is forced into service. If no more paper money were printed than would be sufficient to transact the necessary volume of business on a gold basis, no great harm would be done. But as the confidence of the public in the revolutionary paper money is not so great as its confidence in gold coin, a greater amount of paper has to be issued. This greater issue causes a further reduction in public confidence and a further depreciation in the value of the paper money, which is met by a still larger issue, and so the process continues until the paper money becomes totally valueless. Washington said, truly, that it took a wagonload of the Congressional paper money to pay for a wagonload of provisions. After nearly one hundred and fifty years, the phrase, "not worth a continental," still survives to remind us of the worthlessness of the paper money issued by the Continental Congress. The French as-

signats, being originally issued on the security of the confiscated church lands, held their value for a short time. But
they were presently overissued and became worthless. The
story of the Russian paper ruble is just the same as the
others, but it is so recent that it does not need to be repeated.
It is to be noted that the twin phenomena of paper money
and national debt do not appear in any revolution preceding
the American. But the reason for their non-appearance is
precisely the same as that for the non-appearance of air-
planes or wireless telegraphy. They had not yet been invent-
ed. The first paper money in England was issued in the reign
of William and Mary. The national debt is a little older, if
it be considered as originating at the closing of the exchequer
in 1672. Cromwell had many troubles, but neither national
debt nor inflated currency was among them. The overissue
of paper money is commonly begun during the régime of the
moderate reformers; it continues during the political terror,
but the crisis, the economic terror, involving the total breakdown of the system of exchange, is subsequent to the political terror.

Several causes co-operate to bring the terror to an end.
First, the fear of foreign invaders is dispelled. These armies
have perhaps been driven back sufficiently to remove all
chance of their conquering the nation, and public anxiety
and excitement are greatly abated. The fear of internal revolt dies out when the possibility of foreign aid is removed.
With the defeat of the foreign invaders and suppression of
domestic insurrectionists the occasion of the terror disappears. As the revolutionary rulers build up their army their
power increases and their danger decreases. Finally, with
the defeat of all their open enemies, they are in a situation of
no more danger than any other rulers. In fact, they become

a danger to those who formerly menaced them. But the chief reason for the end of a terror is the emotional exhaustion of the people.

There is a hazy sort of idea in many minds that the reign of terror is invariably brought to an end by the overthrow of the radical revolutionists and the coming into power of moderate men. This idea is entirely false. A terror is generally terminated under the same rulers with whom it began. Cromwell began the Irish Terror and Cromwell ended it. The American Continental Congress began the terror against the Loyalists and also terminated it. The French Convention, which authorized Robespierre, Fouquier-Tinville, and the others to institute the terror, was precisely the same body which afterward executed them for obeying its orders. Gratitude to tools who outlive their usefulness is never characteristic of democratic legislatures. Lenin started the Russian "Red Terror" and Lenin stopped it. He gave Dzerdzinsky another job and changed the Tcheka into an ordinary judicial and secret-service agency of the government. The duration of a terror depends largely upon its violence. The more violent it is, the sooner it is over. The terrors in the English and American revolutions were not violent but they lasted long. The terrors in the French and Russian revolutions were more ferocious and shorter. The French Terror was the shortest. It lasted barely ten months, and it would have been still shorter except for the timidity of the Convention. The republic was in extreme danger only five or six months. The Convention wished to terminate the terror when the danger to the country ceased to be acute, but it was afraid to do so as it believed that public sentiment was still in favor of violence. When it became evident that popular opinion was against the continuation of the terror, the Convention made its agents the scapegoats and executed them as a vicarious sacrifice for its own mistakes. The Red Terror of the Russian Revolution was initiated in response to public opinion. It lasted only so long as effective popular sentiment demanded—about a year.

A terror never ends suddenly. After executions cease, the threats and spying still continue for a considerable time. The tyrannical laws under which a terror operates are repealed only gradually, one by one, over a period of months or even years.

For a long time the energy of the revolutionary government has been concentrated upon turning the whole country into an effective war machine. When the wars are over the job of turning the country back into an effective peace machine proves exceedingly difficult. There is no great wave of popular enthusiasm to help the government in carrying out peacetime policies. The solidarity that comes from danger breaks up. Factionalism appears among the party in power. Public opinion is apathetic. The grafter and the boodler take advantage of the public apathy, and corruption and peculation assume large proportions. It is a great time for the professional politicians with their wire-pulling and their crooked deals. Men who were honest and incorruptible when the Revolution was in danger give way to temptation now that the danger is past. They think they are entitled to recompense themselves at the public expense for their former exertions, and they become dishonest and slack in the performance of their public duties.

As soon as it becomes evident that the revolution is going to succeed, a vast number of "political careerists" crowd into the public service. A political careerist is a person without political convictions who desires to win fame and fortune in politics. So long as the future of the revolution is in doubt he keeps out of sight. As soon as its success is assured, he outdoes all the old revolutionists in his loyalty to revolutionary principles. He adopts the revolutionary phraseology. He joins the party. He attends the caucuses and has himself put on the committees. He gets elected to office and pushes himself forward in every possible way. As he is generally an energetic man as well as a selfish one, he frequently attains to high office, greatly to the detriment of the governmental morale. With governments as with individuals, success is harder on character than failure. The pure idealism of the period of adversity becomes tainted with self-interest after the triumph is won. The conduct of the Rump Parliament after the crowning victory of Worcester, compared to the conduct of the same men during the earlier period of the Revolution, presents a sad picture of moral decline. Men formerly honest and incorruptible filled all the highest posts of the government with their relatives, friends, and dependents, without any regard to the qualifications of these persons for their positions. They became involved in all sorts of dubious jobbery in connection with contracts for government supplies. They neglected their parliamentary business and spent their time and used their positions to further their own private fortunes. When Cromwell at last expelled them, they went out loaded with wealth and with public contempt.

The last end of the American Continental Congress was almost equally devoid of honor. Many of its most efficient members resigned to enter the service of the separate states. Their places were taken by men of small capacity and great rapacity. The powers of the Congress were sufficient to enable it to do much harm without being sufficient to enable it to do much good. Public opinion at last abolished it, but it had ceased to command respect long before it ceased to exist. The last months of the French Convention and the whole period of the Directory presents a similar melancholy picture. Graft, incompetence, and futility are the marks of the time, and they made Napoleon's coup d'état of the Eighteenth Brumaire very easy.

The condition of affairs in Russia after the defeat of Wrangel was bad—though not so bad as the similar period of the French Revolution. The old revolutionary leaders, knowing what to expect, were in some degree ready for the slump when it came. They could not stop its coming, but they mitigated its effects as much as possible. They were not able to prevent graft, but they were merciless to such grafters as they could convict. They shot some and exiled others to Siberia. They could not keep out the political careerists and place hunters, but they held periodic "cleansings" of the public service. The histories and records of all appointees were minutely examined by special committees and all the dubious characters, the so-called "radishes," i.e., those "red" outside but "white" inside, were discharged, so far as they were discoverable. Even with all this effort the slump was a severe one, and the condition of the country was anything but good.

It is a difficult thing to say just when a revolution ends. After the terror and the end of revolutionary warfare the radical party undergoes a transformation. The nature of this change can best be understood by considering the radicals in their aspect as a sect. A sect is a "religious" organization with four chief characteristics: It is at war with the existing moral order. It seeks to establish a new social system different from the one in the midst of which it lives. It makes great use of isolation devices and shibboleths which

isolate it from the rest of the world. It is highly evangelistic
and displays marked missionary zeal. During the time of
revolutionary war the right of the radical faction to exist at
all is denied by the rest of the world. The pagans tried totally to exterminate the early Christians. The Catholics did
their best to kill all the first Protestants. The monarchists
labored to effect the complete extirpation of the original re-
publicans. After the new sect has made good its right to existence, by winning its revolutionary wars, a process of accommodation sets in. The new sect has to be tolerated. Its
validity as an organization for the expression of the four elemental human wishes has to be acknowledged. Its "place in
the sun" must be given it. The general scheme of things
must be so arranged as to allow due weight and influence to
the new institution. On the other hand, the new sect itself
suffers change. Its original ideal of converting the whole
world by revolutionary means suffers a setback. It is forced
to realize that it is not destined to become the sole power on
earth. Its denunciations of the rest of the world lose some of
their fierceness as it gains social recognition and equality of
treatment. Cômpetition with other sects takes the place of
open war. The isolation devices and shibboleths prove great
handicaps now that the sect is one of the great powers of the
earth. So they are gradually abandoned or are enforced
with less rigidity. In their new character as responsible rulers the revolutionists gradually realize that economic and social progress can only be achieved by mutual toleration and
co-operation between themselves and their old-time enemies. So the victors, in spite of themselves, just because
they have won their revolution presently lose most of their
sectarian peculiarities. They cease to be a sect and become a
denomination. A denomination is a broken-down sect, a

"religious" body which acknowledges the right of other bodies to equality with itself. The radicals become tolerant when they have won toleration for themselves.

This process of accommodation goes on until a new working agreement is arrived at. An arrangement is reached whereby the different factions in the revolutionary society have their reciprocal relations defined, and their spheres of action marked out. A new equilibrium is established. The main principles which the revolution has established cease to be matters of controversy. When the process of accommodation has advanced to the point where all the chief factions concerned have compromised enough to make ordinary intercourse between them normally peaceable, the revolution may be said to be at an end.

The Protestant Revolution was over when, in any ordinary community, the Protestant church was built across the street from the Catholic church and the Protestant pastor and the Catholic priest were alike accepted by the general body of citizens as representing normal and ordinary types of religious leadership.

Similarly, the Puritan, American, French, and other revolutions ended when their respective principles gained common recognition. The process was in no instance a rapid one. In the case of all these revolutions some slight traces of imperfect accommodation are still to be seen, while in the case of the most recent great revolution, the Russian, they are well marked. When the foreign foes of a revolution are unable to defeat it, they still delay the formal "recognition" of the new revolutionary government as long as they can. Even after they "recognize" it, they treat its representatives as badly as they dare. Several of Cromwell's first ambassadors to foreign courts were mobbed, and one of them was murdered. All of them were made very uncomfortable until Cromwell, by winning two or three foreign wars, showed that he was not a safe person to treat slightingly. Few of the early American ambassadors to the courts of Europe had a happy time of it. Only fear made the other European nations receive the ambassadors of the revolutionary French Republic, and they were all unmercifully snubbed until the great victories of the revolutionary armies made such snubbing dangerous. Even to this day the ambassadors of the soviet have the "cold shoulder" given them in every capital from Madrid to Peking, while the United States, being the most powerful and most detached nation of all, has been able to dodge formal recognition of the soviet for several years.

But this formal external "recognition" is a matter of much less importance than the reorganization and mutual accommodation which takes place within the revolutionary society itself. The moderate reformers, and later the conservatives, are gradually readmitted to participation in public affairs, functioning as co-ordinate political parties with the radicals. This is done on the tacit understanding (later made explicit) that the new order established by the revolution is to be permanent. The Parliament was admitted by everybody to be supreme in the English system of government. The right of Protestants to have their own form of worship was no longer called in question. The American Republic was acknowledged to be a permanent nation. The soviet was taken for granted as the established form of Russian government. When once these fundamental questions are settled, the business of reconstructing the society goes on easily and rapidly.

The reconstructed social order, in its essential features,

is much like the old system which the revolution aimed to abolish. The new, revolutionary principles are simply fitted into a place in the old scheme of things. Cromwell, even as protector, always held to the theory of the supremacy of Parliament. The Restoration of Charles II did not impair the victory of the Revolution. Charles II never dared to challenge the power of Parliament. He had too vivid a remembrance of his father's fate. When James II did challenge Parliament, he was dethroned in a moment. In the American Revolution, the government finally set up by the Constitution was, even in minute detail, a reproduction of that very English government against which the Revolutionary War was waged. But the basis of the Constitution was the principle, established by the Revolution, that the new government was to be entirely independent of any power except that of its own citizens. The old system was reintroduced, on this understanding, with such alterations as were unavoidable—and no more. In the last end of the French Revolution, those ancient principles of French polity, the centralization of administrative, judicial, and financial powers in the national government and the appointment of local officials by the ministry at Paris, were reintroduced into the government in such a manner that Louis XIV would have recognized them as familiar. But the gains of the Revolution, such as the abolition of feudal privileges and the equality of all men before the law, were carefully preserved. The restoration of Louis XVIII in no way disturbed the victory of the revolutionary doctrines. He did not dare to meddle with the revolutionary settlement as established in law and custom. Later on, the merest attempt of Charles X to return to the *ancien régime* resulted in his immediate dethronement.

It is too soon to say what the future may hold for Russia, but this much may be taken as certain: The supreme power in that country will never again be held by an autocratic czar and an *effete* aristocracy such as existed in 1917. One does not need to be a prophet to assert quite positively that the millions of Russian peasants and proletarians who fought so hard to free themselves from aristocratic and plutocratic tyranny will never again submit their necks to the ancient yoke. It is conceivable, though unlikely, that Russia will again have a czar and an aristocracy. But if so, they will only be the shadow of the old system. Their power and prestige will be small, for any new czardom will lack the wealth which the old one possessed, and which is the only secure basis of control. The estates of the Romanoffs and the other great families have gone forever. Restored monarchies, surrounded by poverty-stricken aristocracies, are never a menace to any revolution. That is why they are tolerated. They are permitted, sometimes, to wear the empty trappings of the old-time authority, but only on condition that they do nothing to disturb the order of things established by the revolution. This great vitality and power of the revolutionary principles is not due to any mysterious virtue which they possess, but, for one thing, to the fact that a large and influential portion of the population have a direct financial interest in maintaining them. Queen Mary I of England had little or no difficulty in getting Parliament to bring back the Roman Catholic church as the state religion, but only on the condition that the pope give up all claim to the millions of acres of church lands confiscated by Henry VIII, and given by him to his nobility and ministers of state.

In the Puritan Revolution what was really at stake was the power to make commercial treaties, levy tariffs, control patent laws, and in general administer the government in the interests of the business men instead of in the interests of monarchical despotism and a landed aristocracy. Once the English bourgeoisie had gained these powers they were quite content to let a king sit on the throne again, provided he did nothing to dispossess them of their new authority, which they used for their own great financial gain. The famous Navigation Act which excluded foreign vessels from commerce with British colonies was passed by the same Rump Parliament which beheaded Charles I. Charles II carefully retained it, as did all the later kings. This act was enormously profitable to British merchants, and was a fruitful source of that discontent in the colonies which produced the American Revolution. The Puritan Revolution was, in short, a struggle by British business men for power to pass laws like the Navigation Act, and the American Revolution was a struggle of American business men to gain the like valuable privilege for themselves. The French bourgeoisie gained this power in their Revolution, and, in addition, the peasants gained possession of the agricultural land of the nation. Neither bourgeoisie nor peasants cared much who ran the government, so long as the political power and the property they gained in the Revolution were secured to them, but these gains depended for their validity upon the formal recognition of the principles of the Revolution.

So the great revolutionary doctrines have been carefully preserved throughout all the subsequent changes in the form of government. France has been twice a kingdom, twice an empire, and three times a republic since 1789, but no change has ever taken place in the power of the bourgeoisie, nor has the land of the peasants ever been in any danger. Similarly, the wars of the Russian Revolution and the history since then seem to show that there does not exist power enough in the world to make the 100,000,000 Russian peasants give back the estates of the nobles, which Lenin divided among them. Even the most reactionary czarist *émigrés* are gradually coming to realize that since the peasant's right to his land rests upon the validity of the principles of the Red Revolution, these principles cannot be successfully questioned. No government has the slightest chance of coming into power in Russia which even so much as hints that the land law of the soviet is not absolutely legal and irrevocable.

It is this economic interest of the preponderant part of the public which carries revolutionary radical government safely through the period of graft, corruption, incompetence, and public apathy which is the characteristic phase after the reign of terror is over and the enemies of the revolution defeated. The weakness and venality of the radical revolutionary government during this phase of revolution is frequently as great as or even greater than that of the original government before the revolution. But the people endure the situation with patience: partly because they are tired of strife and bloodshed, and partly because they know that they have the power in their own hands to remedy conditions peaceably and legally. They are just "waiting for their second wind" before setting themselves to the task.

Generally, though not always, it is the economic situation which arouses them from their lethargy and forces them to take action. The economic weakness and depression become extreme, and the public finances get into a chaotic state. The country is flooded with worthless paper money. Lawlessness shows itself and, with the lawlessness, a reaction against lawlessness on the part of all who have gained through the revolution. Some great leader—Cromwell, Washington, Napoleon, Lenin—is looked to for relief. Formally or informally he leads in a reconstruction of the social order which puts it on a stable and permanent basis. Gradually the more conservative people among those who cherish the revolution come to an understanding, and a new constitution, or a fundamental law of some sort, is proposed. This arouses the bitter antagonism of the more radical revolutionists. There is much public unrest and some turbulence. Finally, the new constitution, or basic law, which largely restores the old pre-revolutionary organization of government, is forced through, though against the fierce opposition of the revolutionary minority. It gradually wins the assent of all factions in the revolutionary society. Many of the *émigrés* return and are granted political rights upon swearing allegiance to the new establishment. The old revolutionary factions subside into political parties, all alike acknowledging the validity of the revolution and supporting the new social order based upon it. The rest of the world gets used to the new order and presently ceases to regard it as dangerous. The revolutionary government itself, as it gets older, ceases to be revolutionary and presently ceases even to think of itself as revolutionary. The revolution is complete.

Just when the Puritan Revolution ended is difficult to say. Popular opinion favors the idea that it ended with the Restoration. The historians are generally agreed that it ended with the Act of Settlement. Doubtless the historians are correct. But, sociologically speaking, the Puritan Revolution did not end on any particular day or even in any particular month or year. It ended when the great mass of ordinary Englishmen agreed that the Parliament was the supreme power in England. It ended when the military antagonism of the Roundheads and the Cavaliers changed into the normal party strife of Whigs and Tories. When that time came, as it did before the end of the seventeenth century, the Revolution was over and the new order established.

The end of the American Revolution can be set only a little more definitely than the Puritan. The military aspect of the Revolution ended, for all practical purposes, with the surrender of Cornwallis. The formal or legal end of the Revolution was the treaty of peace with England in 1783. But the true and actual end was when the average American citizen took the Constitution of 1787 as his normal and permanent system of government. There were many troubles before this time came: Shay's Rebellion and paper money, bickerings between the states, tariff walls of one state against another, and all sorts of hopeless anarchical doings. The people looked to Washington for safety. He, with Madison, Hamilton, and others, urged the formation of a strong national government. This was bitterly opposed by Patrick Henry and other radical revolutionists. The Constitution was finally railroaded by dubious political methods through the various state conventions though a majority of popular sentiment was against it. But it worked successfully, and presently everybody accepted it and became immensely proud of it.

The end of the French Revolution was the coup d'état of the Eighteenth Brumaire, Year VII—November 9, 1799. The same date marks the beginning of the Napoleonic Era. So the histories have it, and there is no occasion to quarrel with them. Yet the real end of the Revolution came when the general body of French people felt assured that the material and moral gains of the Revolution were secure and at the same time that the government was firm and efficient.

This was probably the case a few months after Brumaire. Of the disorganization, distress, financial chaos, and other evils of the period of the Directory it is not necessary to speak. Similarly, the details of Napoleon's coup d'état are of no importance for our purpose. The essential fact is that the majority of Frenchmen wished a strong and able ruler who would ratify and consolidate the revolutionary principles and give permanency to the new powers and property rights of the bourgeoisie and the peasants. They would have been perfectly willing to accept Louis XVIII on that understanding in 1799, just as they did so accept him in 1815. But Louis XVIII tried to bargain for better terms, and the greatest military and political genius of all time seized the opportunity to make himself supreme by complying with the required conditions in the fullest measure. Contrary to an opinion sometimes heard, the wars of the Napoleonic period have no organic connection with the Revolution. No such wars followed any other great revolution. That they followed the French Revolution was due to the mere coincidence that, at the end of this Revolution, the greatest general in history came into power in the most militaristic nation in history. But this situation was altogether exceptional. Great revolutions are normally succeeded by a fairly long period of peace and quiet. The revolutionary society requires time for recuperation. It has had its fill of wars, and wishes to devote itself to the peaceable task of reconstructing a prosperous state on the new foundations laid by the revolution. It will keep the peace unless it is positively forced into war by circumstances over which it has no control. Those persons who expected the Russian Revolution to produce a Napoleon and a whole series of wars were mistaken in their ideas of the revolutionary process. They mistook a

purely accidental and extraneous phenomenon for part of
that process. Napoleon probably did not desire peace, but
even if he had desired it, he could not have obtained it. Pitt
was determined to undo the Revolution and restore the
Bourbons.

The condition of Russia between the defeat of Kolchak
and the adoption of the new economic policy was deplorable.
The country was at peace. Both its foreign and domestic
foes had been defeated, but at terrible cost. The transportation system was almost a wreck. Famine and pestilence rav-
aged the land. The productivity, both of mines and factories, was at a low ebb. The paper money was so depreciated
that the price of a suit of clothes was expressed in figures
which only astronomers are accustomed to deal with. The
government, on the purely political side, was efficient
enough, but the financial and economic life of the country
was anarchical. However, the supreme power was in the
hands of one of the most extraordinary men any revolution
ever produced. The dictator, Lenin, not only ruled the revolutionary radicals, but he ruled the revolutionary conservatives also. He ruled wisely over both and changed what was
necessary when the times required it. The notion that the
communistic system, which prevailed in Russia from 1917 to
1921, was instituted as a bolshevik theory is a legend. Even
the most convinced capitalists would have had to institute
communism in Russia during those years.[1] Russian communism was not the result of theory; it was the result of crisis.
Shipwrecked sailors adrift in an open boat with an insufficient supply of food always institute communism. There is
not enough food for everybody to have what he wants, so
what there is must be equally divided to prevent the stronger

[1] "Russia," *Encyclopaedia Britannica* (13th ed.), III, 420.

from taking more than their share. That was precisely the condition of affairs in Russia for more than three years. If Russia during those years had been governed by Harding and Hoover instead of by Lenin and Trotsky, the communism would have been established just the same. It was not brought in by the bolsheviks, but by the force of circumstances. When the crisis was past Lenin abolished it. Lenin was a convinced communist as many people are convinced Christians. The Christian law is that if a thief steals your coat you are to give him your waistcoat also. It is an ideal law. The Christian believes in it, for what it is—something to be gradually approximated as nearly as may be. But in real life the fact that a man believes in Christian ideals does not prevent him from turning a thief over to the police. Similarly, Lenin was a communist. But he was also a statesman. He recognized that the continuation of communism, after the crisis, was impracticable, and said so. In the face of the fiercest opposition from the extreme radicals of his own party, he reverted to capitalism—state capitalism, but still capitalism. He instituted the new economic policy. Private business for profit was legalized, along with rent and interest on money. Real estate ownership was granted in perpetuity with the right of direct heirs to inherit. Only the great essential industries, such as railroads, mines, forests, and oil wells, were retained under government ownership, and even in these, large concessions were granted to private corporations. Russia ceased to be communistic, or even very socialistic.

The thing everybody demanded, the one thing absolutely essential, was the establishment of an economic order which would safeguard the property rights acquired during the Revolution and at the same time be permanent and

workable. State capitalism met these requirements and so
Lenin established it. The country at once began to recover.
The preposterous paper rubles were retired and a new currency issued which from the beginning was on a par with
gold. The state capitalism established by Lenin proved satisfactory to the vast majority of the Russian people. It exists to this day and in all probability will continue to exist
for generations, irrespective of what political faction admin-
isters the government. The Russian Revolution ended when
the general body of Russian citizens accepted the new economic policy as the normal foundation of everyday life and
took its existence for granted without thinking about it.
That occurred some time during the year 1922 and marked
the end of the Revolution.

Persons not familiar with the history of revolutions sometimes assert that the Russian Revolution ended in failure
because the present Russian government is just as autocratic as the old-time czar'iom. It undoubtedly is so, but in
that respect it runs true to the revolutionary type. A revolution does not diminish the power of a central government in
any essential particular; it rather increases it. Clarendon
was quite correct when he asserted that the Parliament, in
the days of Charles II, was more powerful than Charles I had
ever been, and just as arbitrary. Patrick Henry told the exact truth when he said that the American Constitution gave
the President and Congress more power over the states than
George III and his Parliament had ever exercised over the
colonies. Napoleon was quite as despotic as Louis XIV and
much more despotic than Louis XVI. Lenin was more of a
czar than Peter the Great, and the power now exercised by
the soviet is to all intents the same as that formerly exercised
by the Romanoffs. But a revolution works a real change,

nevertheless. It does not diminish the power of the government, but it does take the exercise of governmental power out of inefficient hands and put it into capable hands. It deposes an incompetent, archaic ruling class and substitutes a competent, up-to-date ruling class. This is a gain. All government is oligarchical, but it makes a difference whether the government oligarchy represents the capable or the incapable classes of society. It is no objection to a government that it exercises authority—that is what it is for. A revolution comes when a government does not exercise authority well.

Another objection made to revolution is that it is a bloody and horrible method of effecting social change—admitting change to be necessary and desirable. The answer to this objection depends upon one's scale of social values. If peace at any price is the *summum bonum*, there is nothing to be said. But if anything in the world is worth fighting for, revolution is better than submission to tyranny. The wars of religion in the sixteenth and seventeenth centuries were certainly very bloody and horrible. Yet it is the consensus of opinion that religious liberty is worth all it cost. Today it is the unquestioned right of every individual to worship as he pleases, or not to worship if he pleases. Rather than part with this liberty the modern man would freely shed his blood.

If it were conceivable that any serious attempt could be made to reintroduce monarchical government into the United States such an attempt would provoke resistance much more bloody than the American Revolution. Rightly or wrongly, the ordinary American citizen considers that his republican form of government is worth many times the blood and treasure spent in the Revolution. In commercial language he is of the opinion that American independence was a fine "buy";

that it has proved a great bargain. Rather than give it up he
would be willing to pay many hundred times what it originally cost. The actual reintroduction of the *ancien régime* into
France is unthinkable today. It would be opposed by ninety-
nine Frenchmen out of a hundred, and opposed to the last
drop of blood. There can be no question that revolutions are
considered worth while. Admitting their costliness, they are
judged to be well worth their price. But there is a larger and
more important question. Have the great historical revolutions, from a rational and scientific, as opposed to an emotional and sentimental, point of view really promoted human
welfare? The question may be stated as a doubt whether
what has been achieved by revolution is true gain. It is a
question as to the validity of certain received judgments
commonly regarded as standing in need of no revision. Admitting that the conversion of the Western World to the
Christian religion was good, was the construction of the
Roman church worth the destruction of the Roman Empire?
Would not the world be better off today if the church had
never become an empire? Would not the energy expended
in making it one have been better spent in the reform of the
secular government? Granting that the monarchical papacy
had a certain value, was that value great enough to compensate for the eclipse of civilization and centuries of brutality
and barbarism? Nobody but partisan religionists would assert that the gain certainly compensates for the loss. From
the point of view of the social welfare, are the futile, squab-
bling sects in a modern town an improvement over the uni-
fied, religious forces of a pre-Reformation town? Was religious anarchy the only alternative to religious tyranny?
One does not need to believe in the infallibility of the pope in
order to see that Protestantism has resulted in the waste and

inefficiency of the religious forces of society. Does not the modern world stand in need of the very religious unity which the Reformation destroyed? Might it not have been better for humanity if the unity of Christianity had been preserved? Has the Reformation resulted in a net social gain? The answer is by no means so easy as the sectarian dogmatist may think. Similarly of the Puritan Revolution. Many people, neither reactionary nor ignorant, question whether the rule of the capitalists has been any improvement over the rule of the kings. They assert that the second despotism has been worse than the first. Is not modern capitalism an apostasy from the true social gospel? Is it not a blind alley leading nowhere? Must not modern civilization retrace its steps in order to get upon the right path once more? Was the tyranny of the plutocrats the only alternative to the tyranny of the kings? These are not foolish questions—or, if they are, more and more people are asking them.

Was it really a social gain when the English-speaking world broke in two in 1776? Is civilization better off today because there are two great English-speaking political units instead of one? Is it not conceivable that human progress might have been greater if the division had never taken place? Suppose the two great sections of the English-speaking people were today united into one great federation with equal rights in all its parts and with its center in America; would not that be a gain? That is what the American Revolution prevented. Did not the American patriots, in their eagerness for a small, immediate good, sacrifice a larger, ultimate good? Has the increase in prosperity been enough to compensate for the increase in provincialism? Was it worth while for George Washington to endure so much for the sake of George Babbitt? Would that fiery Coolidge of revolutionary fame have dumped the tea into Boston Harbor if he could have foreseen Calvin Coolidge?

Nobody can deny that the people of France have gained much good from their great Revolution, but it is certain that they have got much evil also. Admitting that the rule of the aristocrats had to be ended, was it advisable to substitute the rule of the stock jobbers? Is the modern business man really a desirable or an admirable social type? Is he worth all the revolutions it has cost to produce him? It is the answers to such questions as these that will determine the ultimate value of the great revolutions.

SELECTED REFERENCES

BEARD, CHARLES A. *An Economic Interpretation of the Constitution of the United States*, chaps. viii and ix. New York, 1913.

GARDINER, SAMUEL R. *History of the Commonwealth and Protectorate, 1649–1656*, Vol. II, chap. xxv, and Vol. III, chap. xxxi. London and New York, 1903.

———. *A Student's History of England, from the Earliest Times to 1885*, chap. xxvii. London and New York, 1890–91.

HAYES, CARLETON J. H. *A Political and Social History of Modern Europe*, Vol. I, chap. xv. New York, 1922.

ROSS, EDWARD A. *The Russian Soviet Republic*, chap. xxviii. New York and London, 1923.

"Russia," *Encyclopaedia Britannica* (13th ed.), Vol. III.

Russia Today: Official Report of the British Trade Union Delegation, Introduction. London, 1925.

SABINE, LORENZO. *The American Loyalists, or Biographical Sketches of Adherents to the British Crown in the War of the Revolution.* Boston, 1847.

TREVELYAN, GEORGE, M. *England under the Stuarts*, chap. x. London, 1925.

CHAPTER X

THE NEXT REVOLUTION

The preceding study of the revolutionary process has great and obvious faults. The number of revolutions studied has been much too small. The whole series of important secular revolutions in the ancient classical civilization, for instance, has been altogether omitted. Some of these are of great interest and value, particularly the one which changed the Roman Republic into the Roman Empire. Julius Caesar is the ideal secular revolutionist. Some of the great abortive revolutionary movements like the French Jacquerie, Wat Tyler's Rebellion, Jack Cade's Rebellion, and the German *Bauern Krieg* have either not been included at all or have been brought in only incidentally. Certain of the great religious revolutions, Mohammedanism, Methodism, and Mormonism, for example, which present so many strange phenomena, have been ignored. Marginal cases of revolution like Fascism have been passed over. For the most part, only four revolutions have been considered: the English Puritan Revolution, the American Revolution, the Great French Revolution, and the Russian Revolution. But this choice has not been entirely arbitrary. These four revolutions are by common consent the four most important ones which have occurred within the past three centuries. They have all had direct bearing upon the life and thought of Western civilization. They present a wide range of variation, from the mildness of the American to the ferocity of the French; from the piety of the Puritan to the atheism of the

Russian. The variation, indeed, has its limits, but is enough to prevent many chance coincidences. It may be that four strictly contemporary moderate revolutions would make a more useful study: the Austrian, the German, the Hungarian, and the Bohemian.

Not only is the number of revolutions studied too small; many important aspects of revolution have been ignored or slighted. The relation between revolutions and psychic epidemics, religious and linguistic revivals, and mass movements is certainly worth more investigation. Social contagion and the behavior of crowds has been insufficiently examined. The connection between revolution and the mores as well as that between revolution and institutionalism has been very imperfectly brought out. Abortive revolutions and moderate revolutions have been avoided.

With all these faults, and many others, to limit the value of the conclusions, it may seem scarcely worth while to try to draw any. But assured knowledge in this field is very slight. No really objective and scientific study of revolution as a social process has ever been made. Under the circumstances even a purely tentative hypothesis, if based on a fair amount of data, is not without value. Only very provisional conclusions are possible in any case. But even very provisional conclusions are better than total lack of thought and much better than reliance upon popular mythology.

After all due allowances and qualifications have been made, certain facts about revolution appear to be fairly well assured. In the foregoing pages an attempt has been made to show that there is a certain sequence in which the symptoms of revolution make their appearance. Unless this sequence is totally at variance with the facts, a similar sequence, or one somewhat similar, is to be expected in the case of any great revolution in the future. We may take it for certain that revolutions, even violent revolutions, will occur periodically for a long time to come. We hear some talk about substituting peaceable evolution for violent revolution, but such talk is only what the theologians call "pious opinion"—laudable, but imaginative. No technology is being developed for the purpose of translating this talk into action. Modern political science, so called, is much like medieval physical science, largely a matter of incantations, exorcisms, and witch-hunting. Until a serious effort is made to understand revolution, no rational technique for dealing with it can be expected. The great nations employ hundreds of thousands of men and spend hundreds of millions of money on the study of the technique of war. If an equal proportion of the resources of society were expended on the study of the technique of peace, it is possible that we should presently have as well developed a scheme for helping one another as we now have for hurting one another. But "seeking peace and ensuing it" in any such rational and intelligent manner is quite beyond the mental and moral power of any present-day government or nation. Until we have thousands and tens of thousands of competently trained technicians investigating social phenomena with the same zeal and detachment that the physical scientists display in their work, we shall never escape violent revolution. How can a privileged class, which ceases to deserve its privileges, be demoted without war? How can a wealthy class, which ceases to merit its wealth, be made poor without violence? When does a social group cease to be useful and become parasitic? What causes of repression exist in our society? What is repression, and how is it possible at any moment to measure its extent and nature? How much of it is due to economic conditions?

What proportion of the intellectuals feel repression themselves? What proportion are aware of its existence in other classes? We must have the answers to these questions and to many more of the same sort before we can construct any machinery which will be adequate to forestall violent revolution. Modern societies carefully arrange for the study of the Micrococci, the Spirochaetae, the bacilli, and all the other parasitic animal and vegetable organisms; but they carefully avoid the investigation of social parasitism, especially as it affects wealthy and influential classes. The existence of a class of parasites able to live without working, to consume without producing, is seldom recognized as a social disease unless the class is poor. No doubt the idea of the functional test for the ownership of wealth has made some slight advance in late years, but the advance is so slight that it will not affect events greatly for many years to come.

We have practically no scientific machinery for avoiding violent revolution and almost no knowledge of how to construct any such machinery. We shall continue to have violent revolutions until we remedy these deficiencies.

Revolutions will be unavoidable for generations to come because both conservatives and revolutionists have the same way of thinking about society. They are both "standpatters." They both have the concept of a perfect state which is to be preserved inviolate. Their ideals differ, but the attitude of the revolutionist toward his ideal state is exactly the same as the attitude of the 100 per cent American toward the Constitution. The scheme of things which the revolutionist believes in becomes sacred to him through the struggle to attain it. So when his revolution succeeds and his form of social order is in some degree realized, he becomes the strongest of all opponents of further change. The

Russian government is the only one on earth which is more conservative than the American government. Kalinin and Coolidge seem to be persons of precisely the same mentality, and they are both striving to the best of their abilities to do the same thing—that is, to maintain the existing régime in their respective countries. The soviet in Moscow and the Congress in Washington are twin brothers under the skin. The one dominant purpose of both of them is to preserve the *status quo*. Any deviation from the narrow path of rigid conformity is hated by both groups equally. Senator Smoot, excommunicating the heretical Senator La Follette, and Commissar Kalinin, excommunicating the heretical Commissar Trotsky, are as indistinguishable as Tweedledum and Tweedledee. The cabinet of President Coolidge and the cabinet of President Kalinin are as much alike as two flivvers leaving the factory in Detroit.

This fundamental identity of character between the conservatives and the revolutionists is one great reason for the endless succession of revolutions. Revolutionists are not in favor of revolution in general, but only in favor of their own kind of revolution. They do not aim at continuous change, but only at their own amount of change. A world made up of standpatters (whether conservatives or revolutionists) will have revolutions indefinitely because any given revolution merely substitutes a new set of standpatters for an old set. The essential evil about both groups is that they are *fundamentalists*. Only their repentance and conversion to the doctrine and practice of scientific social *evolution* can bring revolutions to an end. Of such repentance and conversion there is as yet little sign.

If future revolutions are unavoidable, can we predict anything as to the time when the next revolution will take place? So far as the United States is concerned, it would seem to be possible to make a reliable prophecy. If the previously given analysis of the development of revolution is at all in accord with the facts, it is certain, almost to the point of mathematical demonstration, that there is no possibility of a violent revolution in the United States within any future that need cause concern to persons now alive. The immediate symptoms of revolution are entirely absent from our society. The remote symptoms, if they exist at all, are so slight as to be unrecognizable. The enormous majority of the American people are not only content with the social order in which they live, but they are enthusiastically loyal to it and inordinately proud of it. Such discontent as exists is superficial and transitory. In regard to the volume of dissatisfaction, no equally numerous society ever had so little. No economic incentive to revolution and no new social myth are anywhere discoverable. The intelligentsia are prosperous and happy. All the other social groups are in the same condition. No such complacent, self-satisfied, and universally contented society has existed in Western civilization since the days of the Flavian emperors of Rome. The radicalism of the United States is more conservative than the conservatism of any other great nation. An ultra-conservative British cabinet would be considered radical in Washington. This country is, with the exception of Russia, the most conservative country on earth. It is without exception the most prosperous nation in the world. This does not mean that no violent revolution will take place in the future. It very certainly does mean that no such revolution will take place within the next two, or even the next three, generations.

The next American revolution will not occur in the twentieth century. The more one studies the symptoms of revolution, the more reliable does this prediction appear to be. The more carefully one scrutinizes our contemporary society, the stronger becomes the conviction that it is destined to remain firm and stable for a long time to come. The periodic "scares" of revolution which afflict the American people are baseless and childish. A great revolution did take place in Russia recently, but conditions in Russia were totally and fundamentally different from those in the United States. All of the symptoms of revolution were fully developed in Russia; they are completely absent in the United States. It is exceedingly doubtful whether there are fifty thousand persons in the United States who really desire a violent revolution. There were more than fifty million people in Russia ready to go to any extreme in order to overthrow the ruling class and confiscate their property. A despotic monarchy, a haughty aristocracy, a corrupt state church, poverty, ignorance, disease, all in their most aggravated form, sum up the situation which existed in Russia before the Revolution. The best way to define the United States would be to say that it is the country where these evils either do not exist at all, or exist in the smallest degree. There is no more reason for Americans to become alarmed at the Russian Revolution than for the people of Florida to become alarmed at an eruption of Vesuvius. Yet, owing to the general ignorance of the nature of social upheavals, the people of the United States have developed marked cases of "nerves" in connection with revolution and revolutionary propaganda. Revolutionary propaganda is perfectly harmless in any community where social conditions are healthy. The public nervousness in the United States has been repeatedly exploited by professional politicians for their own purposes. The result has been that

many thousands of humble, innocent, and useful foreign laborers have suffered undeserved hardship, imprisonment,
and terrorization. The possibility of the recurrence of all
this needless suffering is by no means remote. It is the duty
of well-informed people to prevent such an injustice by every
means in their power. We have not much real knowledge of
revolutions, but what we have is abundantly sufficient, if
properly used, to prevent such "scares" as we have recently
had. A little light on the subject would bring great relief to
multitudes of ordinary people, both Americans and foreigners, who are the victims of such "scares." The only losers
would be a small group of self-seeking politicians and professional terror-mongers who capitalize popular ignorance
and credulity.

If the next American revolution is at least three generations in the future and probably more, is it possible to predict anything as to its nature? If we had only American
data to go on, the task would be practically impossible. But
we have other data. All countries which have experienced
the Industrial Revolution show a remarkable uniformity of
development. The Industrial Revolution began in England
in the latter half of the eighteenth century. In due course
appeared slums and palaces, sweatshops and private yachts,
trusts and trade unions, and hundreds of kindred phenomena. The Industrial Revolution came to America about fifty
or sixty years later than it did to England. The subsequent
developments appeared, similarly, fifty or sixty years later.
Whether we take child labor, factory inspection, hours of
work, union organization, political action on the part of capital and labor, foreign investments, foreign trade, or anything else, we find that this generalization holds good to an
astonishing degree. Unless the trend of history for one hun-

dred and fifty years is to be reversed (of which there is no
sign) we may be fairly certain that within the next two or
three generations a political labor party with socialistic tendencies will appear in the United States—very much such a
party as now exists in Great Britain. Due allowance must be
made for the difference between natural resources and population in the two countries. Great Britain, compared to her
natural resources, has a far greater population than the United States. Allowance must also be made for the time necessary to Americanize our foreign workmen. But when everything is discounted that needs to be, it still seems true that
this country, in common with all others in which the Industrial Revolution has developed, is destined to evolve through
capitalism into some sort of social control of industry. The
democratic trend in Western civilization has been continuous for more than four centuries. There have been temporary ebbs and apparent setbacks, but these have not changed
the direction of the main movement. We already have religious and political democracy, and it is most unlikely that
the democratic trend will cease until we have industrial democracy also. Industry is the last stronghold of autocracy.
If the people of the United States do not like the President
of the United States they can get rid of him at the next election, but if the people of the United States do not like the
President of the United States Steel Company there is nothing they can do about it. If American citizens object to the
size of their tax bills they can get relief, but if they object to
the size of their gasoline bills, or coal bills, or meat bills, they
cannot get relief—at present. The taxes which industry im-
poses upon the public are not yet regulated, or only to a minor degree. It seems certain that the demand for further
regulation of industry in the interests of labor and the public

will continue. If the ballot should fail to secure this, resort will be had to direct action, to strikes. If that should fail, the public will follow the example of the "Patriots of 1776" and get what they want by revolution.

It has long been an essential part of a British prime minister's job to negotiate with labor unions. Frequently the British labor unions dictate to the political Parliament. The only escape from this tyranny lies in socializing the machines. If the public will not assume the ownership and control of the machines, then the labor unions probably will. In either case there will be a revolution. There are optimists like Professor Carver[1] who believe that the revolution will be peaceable. The labor unionists and the general public as individuals will buy out all the capitalists, and everybody will be happy. However, it is open to doubt whether Professor Carver's optimism is based upon any very extensive study of revolutions. Let us suppose that by years of industry and frugality the labor unionists acquire one-third of the industrial wealth of the nation. They will then be intelligent enough and powerful enough to take the other two-thirds by direct action. Perhaps they will not do so, but the history of labor unions affords little ground for crediting them with such extreme self-abnegation. The Russian peasants were supposed to be unusually stupid persons, but after they had acquired one-third of the agricultural land of Russia by peaceful means they took the other two-thirds by revolution. The French peasants did the same thing. It may be that American workingmen are more scrupulous than European peasants. Nevertheless, scruples about property rights have never, historically, proved strong enough to prevent any social group from taking wealth by violence, so soon as it was

[1] T. N. Carver, *The Present Economic Revolution in the United States.*

able to do so. When the labor unions attain the strength to confiscate the industrial wealth of the country, an excuse for doing so will not long be lacking. Practically all the land in the United States was, no long time ago, taken from its ancient owners, the Indians, by force or chicanery. How many of the great American fortunes will stand rigid examination of the methods by which they were accumulated—particularly if they are judged by the standards of a revolutionary society? The vast estates of many a great English noble were obtained by the spoliation of the church. It is not probable that the labor unionists will prove different from other classes who in time past have utilized their opportunities to acquire wealth by violence.

On the other hand, it is unlikely that the general body of the American people will long submit to the despotism of the labor unions. The power of the unions will become great, yet it can never equal the power of the whole society. But in order to exercise power over the instruments of production, society will have to assume—has already, in fact, begun to assume—a control which approaches ownership. So we may come to state capitalism as the alternative to syndicalism. For a while there may probably be a situation much like that now taking shape in England. Two equal and independent authorities, the political Parliament and the labor-union Congress, will struggle for supreme power. The victory must rest at first with the labor Congress, but at last with the public. The final result will be some sort of compromise. Political government will probably always be necessary, in spite of all the dreams of the syndicalists; and the political and the economic control of society must be in some way coordinated. The guild socialists have envisaged this problem correctly enough, whether they have found a solution or not. No class, we may be sure, will permanently be allowed to exercise power over society without being responsible to society for the way that power is exercised. In the economic sphere the problem of enforcing such responsibility on either capital or labor has not yet been worked out. Apparently it cannot be worked out. Must it be fought out by revolution?

SELECTED REFERENCES

BÜCHER, CARL. *Industrial Evolution*. Translated from the 3rd German ed. by S. MORLEY WICKETT. New York, 1907.

BREYSIG, KURT. "Der wirtschaftliche Fortschritt und die Aufgaben einer geschichtlichen Entwicklungsmechanik," *Schmollers Jahrbuch*, Vol. XXXVI, 1912.

BURNS, CECIL DELISLE. *The Principles of Revolution; a Study in Ideals*. London, 1920.

CARVER, T. N. *The Present Economic Revolution in the United States*. Boston, 1925.

COLE, GEORGE D. H. *Guild Socialism: A Plan for Economic Democracy*. New York, 1921.

FOLLETT, MARY P. *The New State*. New York, 1918.

LE BON, GUSTAVE. *The World in Revolt; a Psychological Study of Our Times*. New York, 1921.

MACDONALD, JAMES RAMSAY. *Parliament and Revolution*. New York, 1920.

MICHELS, ROBERT. *Political Parties: a Sociological Study of the Oligarchical Tendencies of Modern Democracy*. New York, 1925.

———. *Sozialismus und Fascismus in Italien*. Munich, 1925.

NICEFORO, ALFREDO. "Massstäbe der Überlegenheit und des Fortschritts einer Zivilisation," *Jahrbuch für Soziologie*, I (1925), 239–56.

PARK, ROBERT E., AND BURGESS, ERNEST W. *Introduction to the Science of Sociology*, chaps. xiii and xiv, "Collective Behavior and Progress." Chicago, 1923.

PAUL, EDEN AND CEDAR. *Creative Revolution*. London, 1920.

WALLACE, ALFRED RUSSEL. *The Revolt of Democracy*. New York and London, 1914. ·

WIESER, FRIEDRICH. *Das gesetz der Macht*. Wien, 1926.

WOLFE, ALBERT B. *Conservatism, Radicalism and Scientific Method: An Essay on Social Attitudes*. New York, 1923.

INDEX

INDEX

Adams, Samuel, 43, 79, 142

Agitators, 24

Albigenses; and the papacy, 7, 61

American Journal of Sociology, 2

American Revolution: state of society in 1776, 30; and government under George III, 36; and publicists, 43; and attacks on repressors, 51; and George III's folly, 66; economic incentive of, 79; and the social myth, 94; and Committee of Safety, 110; shibboleths of, 114; and moderate reformers, 117; and Tories, 123; and crime, 136, 137; and era of optimism, 140; release of political prisoners, 141; coalition government in, 142; military government in, 147; radicalism in, 151; changing leaders in, 157; denunciation of, 159; and military dictatorship, 165; insurrections against, 171; reign of terror in, 180; confiscation of property in, 187; corruption in, 191; end of, 194, 201; and reconstruction, 196; real issue of, 198; as a social gain, 208. *See* Revolution

Bacon's Rebellion, 62

Bakunin, 26

Bauern Krieg, 103, 105, 210

Beggars, sturdy: their appearance before revolutions, 27

Boston Tea Party, 102, 106

Burke, Edmund, *Plea for Conciliation*, 54

Calvin, John, 42; and usury, 87; and social myth, 93

Capitalism: power of, 6; and labor unions, 6; and modern society, 8; and exploiters, 39; and Calvin, 88; and Lenin, 204, 208

Carver, T. N., 219

Charles I, 29, 33, 35, 45, 59, 105, 111, 117, 138, 142, 157, 171, 179, 198

Christians, 53; and pagans, 56; as chosen people, 58, 60; and economic incentive, 74; and attitude toward wealth, 88; and "millenial hope," 89; and the social myth, 92; and isolation devices, 113; and moderate reformers, 118; and patriotism, 122; law of, 204

Communism, Russian, 203 ff.

Conservatives: rôle in revolution, 119; treatment of by revolutionists, 121; in Hungarian and Prussian revolutions of 1848, 128; in Russian Revolution of 1905, 128; confiscation of property of, 186; and reconstruction, 195

Constitution, American, 196

Crime waves: 28; in time of revolution, 136

Cromwell, Oliver: 33, 107, 142, 151, 157, 164, 177-78, 187, 189, 191, 194, 196, 200; and the commonwealth, 42

Crowds: psychology of, 99; function of in revolutions, 101; personnel of, 102; uniformity of, 102 ff.; and Boston Tea Party, 102; and storming of Bastille, 105; and the shibboleth, 112; in reign of terror, 183

Darwin, *Origin of Species*, 21

Das Kapital, 95

Despotism: of Lenin, 108; in revolutions, 121; of majority, 132

INDEX